Schooling
Exercises in-hand

Working towards
suppleness and confidence

Schooling Exercises in-hand

Working towards
suppleness and confidence

Oliver Hilberger

CADMOS

Disclaimer

Neither the author, the publisher nor any others involved directly or indirectly in the creation of this book can accept any liability for accidents or damage of any kind that may occur as a result of practising the exercises detailed here.

In this book, riders are shown not wearing riding hats. Readers should always ensure that the appropriate safety equipment is worn: sturdy footwear and gloves when undertaking in-hand work, and when riding, a riding hat to the relevant recommended safety standard, riding boots or shoes, gloves and if necessary a body protector.

Imprint

Copyright © 2011 Cadmos Publishing Limited, Richmond, UK
Copyright of original edition © 2008 Cadmos Verlag GmbH, Munich, Germany
5th edition 2019

Design and setting: Ravenstein + Partner, Verden.
Photography and Drawings: Pamela Sladky
Translation: Claire Williams
Copy-editor: Christopher Long
Printed by: www.graspo.com

British Library Cataloguing in Publication Data

A catalogue record of this book is available from the British Library.

Printed in EU

ISBN 978-3-86127-964-8

www.cadmos.co.uk

Contents

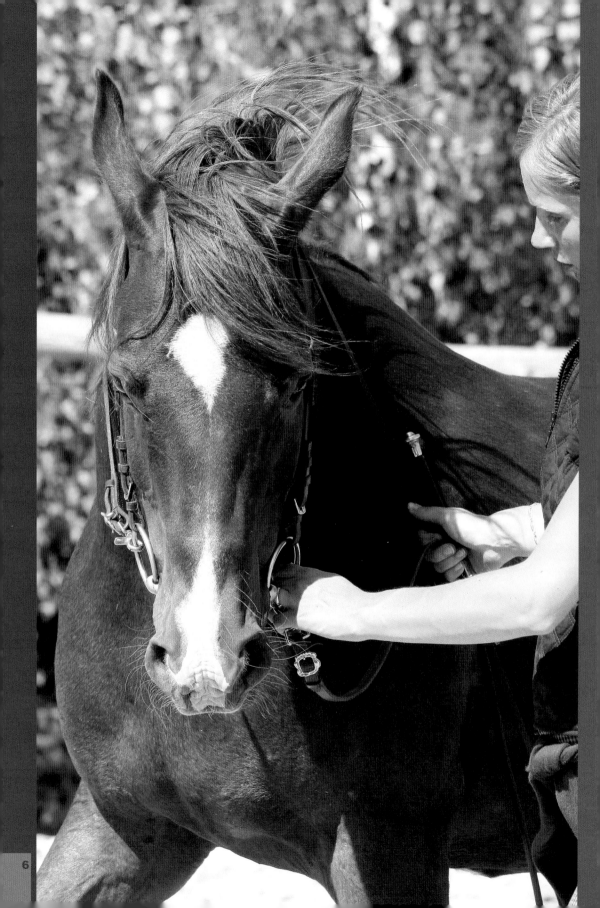

The horse in movement 53

Shoulder-in 91

Renvers 107

Travers 115

Half-pass 123

Introduction

The history books first record of in-hand work is in the sixteenthth century. Antoine de Pluvinel introduced work in pillars to the repertoire of training methods for horses. Work in hand continued to develop until the beginning of the twentieth century, when it reached its peak with François Baucher.

Subsequently the demands of the cavalry suppressed virtually all in-hand work to the point of extinction. It was only in the centres of equitation such as the Spanish Riding School in Vienna, the Cadre Noir in France, and the Andalucian School of Equestrian Art in Spain, where in-hand work was continued and to this day has a permanent role in the training of horses.

The pressure to perform and common conventions often portrayed in-hand work in a poor light. It has been dismissed as a fallback for those who can't ride; a horse seems to be recognised as such only when it has a saddle on its back. The fact is, however , that no horse is born with a rider on its back, and no person is born as a perfect rider . For this reason alone, in-hand work offers a valuable alternative and extension to riding.

It is true that the repertoire of classical equitation offers many different exercises and movements; however, for the majority of riders these are not accessible, or are attainable only after many years of training. In addition there are some horses that can't be ridden at all, or only to a limited extent due to illness or advancing age, yet still need to be worked carefully. Conventional lungeing reaches its limits very quickly, whilst working a horse in-hand can build up certain individual muscles in a targeted manner and so contributes significantly to a quick recovery or a longer healthy life.

And an additional point: winter poses certain hard challenges for riders trying to continue working horses under saddle. The ground is often covered in snow or frozen solid, and not everyone has an indoor school at their disposal. And even when conditions outside are good, many riders fall into a monotonous work pattern with their horses which at some stage ends up in a lack of motivation or enjoyment when schooling or hacking out. In all of these cases, in-hand work offers a sensible solution.

Regardless of one's riding ability, the exercises in this book of fer anyone a practical

The horse trained in-hand will also be smooth and supple to ride.

approach to flexing and supplying a horse, preparing him for more advanced movements. In-hand work offers not only an alternative to, but an extension of riding.

Transforming your horse

The average leisure rider normally has only one horse. Her own horse! She invests a lot of time and money in her hobby and is above all emotionally tied to it. It is therefore sensible to give quite a bit of thought to keeping the four-legged friend healthy. Working in-hand can make a considerable contribution to this. Very often you think you know your own horse with all his strengths, weaknesses and characteristics – in short with his own character, that makes every horse so unique. If you start to train your horse using in-hand work, he will very quickly develop – not only physically, but mentally. Lazy horses will become more active, tense horses will become calmer, and above all his self-confidence will grow.

Alongside your horse, you will be astonished at the transformation, for he will contribute more and more to the work being asked of him, with ever-growing suppleness and flexibility. The horse needs to be given the chance to develop himself to the full within a broader framework. Even very low-ranking horses can blossom and develop their own sense of pride.

If you have the opportunity to improve your own horse's quality of life, use it. In-hand work offers this chance.

Even lower-ranking horses can reach unexpected heights, thanks to in-hand training.

EACH HORSE IS DIFFERENT

No one horse moves exactly like another – for this reason it is pointless to expect your horse to imitate exactly the movements of the horses illustrated in this book. This book is structured in such a way that you will be able to follow each phase in the training step by step, so that you can get the same idea across to your horse. Despite this, there will be differences. You must try and set your own priorities, so that repeating an exercise for one horse is incredibly important, for another not. It is a particular challenge to recognise these nuances and use them for your own horse – thus success becomes all the more significant.

Suppling and gymnasticising:
the main purpose of in-hand work

Playing with balance

Anyone who has anything to do with horses must at some stage come across the terms 'suppling' or gymnasticising. But what does it mean to gymnasticise your horse?

In recent years, fortunately, even amongst leisure riders, an awareness has developed that every horse can benefit from suppling work. Lateral movements are not, by a long shot, exclusive to dressage. As a leisure rider, you may not have to compete, nor are there any rules or regulations that you have to follow. Your rules are laid down by your horse. But it is the responsibility of the rider to keep her horse supple and flexible, so that if at all possible, it continues to be able, even at an advanced age, to carry a rider without pain or injury to his joints.

For a horse, every change in direction, speed or pace involves a change of balance. That means that only by moving his centre of gravity can a horse carry out certain movements and react accordingly to this change of balance.

A horse that is fleeing from danger transfers his weight towards his shoulders, whilst a cornered or trapped horse will put all his weight into his hindquarters, and rear up to defend himself.

Watching horses playing in the field offers a good opportunity to see how in their interplay the transfer of balance is involved in both attack and defence. Effortlessly and with enjoyment they train their reflexes, muscles, skill and sense of balance. In their daily games they are keeping themselves supple in order to (albeit in principle only) give themselves an advantage in the struggle for survival over their enemies, or as a stallion to win himself his own herd of mares.

The inclination to exercise and maintain suppleness is built into the horse by nature – the best possible prerequisite for us as trainers to be able to develop and support this characteristic.

From a horse's point of view there is an even more important point that comes into effect: with improving suppleness, muscular development and weight-bearing capacity, a psychological change will also take place in the horse. He will become stronger, more self-confident

The self-confident horse – he is growing from the inside and outside.

and more aware of how to use his new skills. With every exercise a horse will become more agile, confidence in his own body will grow, balance will improve and the weight-bearing capacity be trained. The more his hindquarters are trained, the more his balance will be transferred back and down towards his haunches. An interaction takes place between the state of body and state of mind: the flight instinct will increasingly recede, being pushed away from the shoulders, and the horse's self-confidence will grow and from the horse's point of view will become the objective of his gymastic exercises.

Dressage has made it its business to cultivate, refine and develop the horse's natural move-ments. For every physical position there is a matching emotion. A horse in collection has a different psychogical condition to the horse grazing in a field. The starting point is thus the horse's mood, expressed through his physical being.

The aim and intention of any dressage rider is the training of a horse to the highest level of perfection. The true expression of this for any horse is when the enjoyment of his own movement, self-confidence and pride are expressed through High School movements.

As a leisure rider, however, it is not dressage, but rather gymnastic exercises that should be the focus of attention. Gymnastic exercises that make sense to the horse, that the horse understands and have a side effect of enabling him to be able to carry his rider effectively. From this point of view it is a relatively easy way to strengthen and to train your horse. Gymnastic exercises 'empower' the horse, facilitating the development of his ability , animating his movements with emotion, and developing his will to build up his strength.

Through experience, observation and science, people long ago discovered how a horse can be exercised gymnastically: turning, bending, shoulder-in, half-pass, piaffe – all are terms that have been created and that dressage riders now understand as 'movements'. Every rider knows that the horse's body is really not made to carry a load on his back. A horizontal spine doesn't make the best weight-bearing platform. Thus man has to intervene in order to help the horse. Unfortunately this 'help' often deteriorates into brute force, and has the opposite effect to that intended. Instead of exercising the horse, you restrict and upset it.

What would happen though if the horse set his own rules? For consideration first of all would be physical factors such as age, build, conformation faults, stage of development and musculature. As the trainer of your horse, you must learn to recognise and to decide what does your horse good and what has a good effect on his body, muscles, joints and tendons. What does he find easy, where does he need more help? What should you watch out for, so that you don't cause your horse harm?

The second point to consider is the mental factor: character, mood and experience – in short, his interior. Is it, for example, sensible to chase a nervous horse round the manege at a flat-out gallop? If the horse sees a point to the gymnastic exercises, then everything will suddenly become much easier! Shoulder-in will then not only be a movement in a dressage test, but rather an effective means to strengthen the hindquarters, for building muscles and, not least of all, a further step towards a proud, self-confident and healthy horse that will stay fit into old age. The beneficial side-effect for the rider is that the horse will be strengthened in such a way that he is able to bear more weight on his back – without pain, without long-term harm, without wanting to escape or run away. Of course it is possible to further develop and refine these movements and take them through to their ultimate conclusion, but it will never degenerate into a soulless exercise. Dressage ridden on the basis of gymnastic exercises designed with the horse first and foremost in mind can become a wonderful experience for the horse.

"When the horse is brought into selfcarriage, when he wants to show himself off to his best advantage, you have attained a riding horse that is happy and magnificent, proud and worth watching."

This oft-quoted sentence is from the Greek riding master Xenophon's masterpiece, *The Art of Horsemanship*. Does he not expressively describe the essence of gymnastic exercises? Mankind can help the horse to take up the most beautiful of positions. Happy, magnificent and proud – emotions that cannot be forced. To achieve this, a foundation must be built, from which everything else stems. Working in-hand offers just such a foundation.

But what exactly can gymnastic exercises achieve in detail?

In play you don't have to work to achieve suppleness – it comes all by itself.

Well, they encourage:
• suppleness
• agility
• muscle development
• balance
• self-confidence.

Be supple and relaxed

One of the great advantages of working in-hand over riding, is that you as the trainer and handler are in the horse's field of vision. Alone, your presence gives the horse a certain degree of security and leadership.

Who hasn't experienced the following? You are on your horse when he shies at something – a rustling noise, an unexpected object, or in many cases an unknown 'something'. The horse absolutely refuses to go forward. At best he stays standing exactly where he is; in the worst case he does an about-turn and bolts in the opposite direction.

Any attempt to get the horse past the object of fear – whether by voice, whip or spurs – fails. Instead, if you get of f and lead your horse past the source of danger, you will mostly very quickly overcome his fear.

But what is happening here? When the horse shies, the rider unknowingly also tenses his own muscles. The horse feels this, feels that his own fear is confirmed, and one reaction leads to another. As soon as the rider has got over his first shock, annoyance sets in, meaning the rider's muscles can't relax again, and the horse does not relax himself.

If the rider dismounts though, and steps into the horse's field of vision, one of the reasons for agitation – the rider in the saddle – is immediately overcome. Usually the horse is happy to follow his rider, who he has accepted as being a higher-ranking member of his herd. In addition, the horse now has a 'shield' in front of him to protect him from the supposed danger. The tension has disappeared, his rider exudes the calmness that the horse at such moments needs, and gives him the lead. Thus the horse overcomes his fear.

Through this sense of security a horse will settle down again much faster. The muscle tension will disappear, and he reverts back to even balance – from tension to relaxation.

Taking the rider from the horse's back removes one of the possible causes of tenseness. *Suppleness and relaxation* is the basic requirement for effective and productive work. It can be achieved much faster through working in-hand than by riding. Supple muscles enable the horse to complete movements that train and help supple the entire body.

Muscle development

A relaxed, supple horse will within a short time build-up exactly those muscles that he needs in order to carry himself and his rider without difficulty. Whether in a dressage arena, or hacking out, only a strong musculature can bear the weight of a rider over a period of time and support a horse's joints, tendons and ligaments.

In-hand work offers the opportunity to prepare a horse in the best possible way for this additional burden. The muscular system is able to develop, the horse will feel better working in the correct position, as with increasing strength it will become easier for him to carry himself. Every lesson will be carried out with increasing ease, the horse will find himself in a positive cycle of development, leading to a happy, satisfied and healthy life.

Balance

Every horse is by nature one-sided – just as every person is right- or left-handed. A dressage rider struggles with this crookedness over the horse's entire life. This will probably not make as much of an impression on the leisure rider – the problems caused by one-sidedness are expressed more in a difficulty to turn in a particular direction, to canter on the correct lead, or a tendency to favour one rein.

A horse that favours the left will prefer to canter on the left rein, cut corners on the right rein and he will find it difficult to bend around the right leg. In such a horse the centre of balance is over his right shoulder – i.e. it is transferred to the right.

By working in-hand, it is possible very quickly and effectively to even up this imbalance, both physically and psychologically. From the saddle you have not only to fight against the horse's natural instinct to flee, but also this one-sidedness. If you are standing next to him on the ground, however, you can concentrate totally on this unevenness.

As explained at the outset, every exercise or movement involves moving the horse's centre of gravity: to the left, to the right, forwards or backwards. Working in-hand, you also have the chance to directly lead and influence this – and to directly benefit from this when in the saddle.

How important the time spent working on straightness is and the correct balance arising out of it will show itself in collected work. Even with a horse showing great talent for High School work, if you neglect the basic principles of straightness and the suppling work that goes with this, he will become steadily more crooked throughout his life.

Body awareness

Training your horse to develop an improved awareness of his body is an essential area in which in-hand work can particularly prove its advantages. As his trainer, you can show your horse with the following exercises exactly what should be done. You are giving your four - legged partner the chance to listen to his own body. He is given the opportunity to feel and be aware of his own hindquarters. The horse notices exactly what part of his body is being exercised, and will start to be more aware of his body; his balance will be transferred and through this the training starts to have a purpose.

In the case of larger warmbloods with long necks and long legs, they may be big moving but because of the way they are built, at the beginning of their training, they often encounter problems with co-ordination of their bodies and how to best use their quarters. If they are tending towards 'pacing' in walk (i.e. two-beat instead of four-beat) then the work in-hand, and particularly the work involved in lateral movements, works wonders in correcting these problems with rhythm in order to keep the paces true.

Self-confidence

There is an important central element in training a horse – that of self-confidence. Suppleness is developed from the start, smoothness, muscular development, improved balance and a developing awareness of his own body will form a new world for any horse. He will practise the lessons with ease and with joy in the movement, whether in the manege or out hacking – the work done in-hand will close the circle in order to open a new one: perhaps with a rider in the saddle?

The demands on the human partner are somewhat more modest. If you approach in-hand work with no preparation whatsoever, then a lot can go wrong. Suddenly you will find yourself within easy reach of his head, teeth, body and hooves. One prerequisite for productive and safe work with your horse is therefore mutual respect, which must of course be earned.

In human society there are many unwritten social rules which must be respected in order not be on the receiving end of someone else's disapproval. One example of this is the rule of

A true partnership can develop on a foundation of mutual respect.

personal space. When people meet there will always be a certain physical distance maintained between each person. Each respects the personal space of the other, and only particular friends or relatives may cross this invisible boundary. If a stranger crosses this line, then you quickly feel uncomfortable, may find this closeness obtrusive or aggressive, and will step back.

Horses too have this feeling of personal space, which may only be broken into by special friendships. Mostly they respect the individual space of their herdmates, with too much proximity leading to a feeling of unwellness, withdrawal or even aggression.

Most people view it as natural that they can automatically intrude into a horse's own personal space, although this may be very uncomfortable for the horse himself. He will therefore notice it when this invisible line is suddenly observed and respected, and this is what leads to the growth of a true sense of respect. But of course the same rule applies to your horse! As a person, I have my own personal space, that must be accepted by my horse. The horse may also not intrude into this space in an aggressive or obtrusive manner.

When the horse is aware that his human observes and respects this rule, then for the future it matters not who is the stronger and who the weaker in the partnership. Mutual respect will develop in such a way that it would never occur to the horse to cross this line with force.

When working in-hand, you are in close proximity to the horse. You are therefore immediately stepping into his personal space. The distance between you both is so small that it could be viewed as an intrusion. For this reason it is especially important to act with particular sensitivity. You must pay attention that you behave with respect, calmness and no fuss, and yet remain firm in your demands. In return, however, you are giving up your own personal space and should expect exactly the same treatment from your horse that you give to him.

Clarity and precision are the essential prerequisites that the handler must bring to working in-hand. This will only happen when you know exactly what you are doing. This assuredness will come only with knowledge, experience and time.

What's in it for you?

The work done in-hand also offers riders a range of benefits. A rider can develop:
• understanding
• clarity of vision
• co-ordination
• fitness
• self-control.

As the handler, you must first of all learn and understand how you can best help the horse to learn: which movements can put the horse in this or that balance? Which changes to his centre of balance can be achieved by this or that aid? When is the horse moving correctly? When does a horse train particular muscle groups? With which exercise can you influence a specific hind leg? And most importantly, how do you co-ordinate the reins, whip and your own body so that the correct aids are given?

One prerequisite of communicating with your horse is understanding. In-hand work is a means to an end, rather than an end in itself. When the trainer knows exactly what she does, and why she does it, then the horse will understand much faster and be able to follow the commands given.

The work in-hand therefore offers an immense advantage: as the person positioned next to the horse, you just about always have everything in sight. You see the responses to the aids, you see his head, neck, back and hindquarters. You are therefore able at the same time to train your own eye. The many pictures in this book will also help you with this. And once you have learnt the skill of observation from the ground, you can use this experience to benefit as a rider.

Finally, only those who recognise when a lesson or movement has been carried out well are able to give praise at the right moment or make the necessary correction. With this positive reinforcement, any intelligent being can be helped to reach the highest level of achievement.

"The horse is your mirror.
It never flatters you.
It reflects your mood.
It also mirrors its changes.
Never get annoyed with your horse,
for you can just as well get
annoyed with your mirror."

What Rudolf Binding describes in these words should be taken to heart by every rider. Unjustified punishment leads to a lack of under - standing, in the case of any living creature, not just the horse. As a person, you should always have your negative emotions under control when around your horse. Self-control is a prerequisite for being able to think clearly. Horses have a fine sense for a person's mood. Unspoken praise will still be recognised as such, if the trainer is pleased about something. On the other hand, any horse will also recognise pent-up negative energy. This tension causes tenseness in the horse very quickly, the atmosphere is disturbed and productive work is only possible with difficulty.

On days like this don't even start to work, as your horse should never be seen as a valve through which you can let off steam or get rid of stress. It is better instead just to hack out for a relaxing ride, or simply give him a thorough grooming.

Equipment

Lungeing cavesson

Protection for the horse's mouth, an aid when leading and lungeing, basic equipment for work done from the ground and indispensable for the training of a youngster – the opportunities and advantages for the use of the lungeing cavesson are well-known to most riders. Variations range from the thickly padded, heavy German versions to the shiny, serated metal model of the Spanish *serreta*.

The lungeing cavesson has a long tradition in Europe. Riding Masters such as Federigo Griso, Antoine de Pluvinel or François Robichon de la Guérinière appreciated the advantages of the lungeing cavesson, which they used in their daily work with horses. Whilst in southern Europe, through the working equitation of the Vaqueros and Guardians, the lungeing cavesson is still part of the tack used up to current times, in Central Europe riding as a sport developed in such a way that this piece of tack had no further place. A not inconsiderable part of this lay with the development of the drop noseband as a varition of the cavesson, combining as it did to have an ef fect through both the noseband and bit.

The thickly padded German lungeing cavesson can be recognised by the fact that it lies very softly on the horse's nose. On the one hand its effect is weakened somewhat through this softness, but on the other hand it forgives a beginner making mistakes with the hand. The signals given through the reins though come with rather less precision through to the horse's nose.

The thick padding acts as a buffer; unsteadiness will not be so quickly passed on and unintended half-halts will have no lasting negative effects on your communication with the horse. The nose is protected so the horse cannot have too much pressure exerted on this area. In the case of what is often quite a substantial piece of tack, the argument is often used that it is not suitable for the purpose of education and training. It is often labelled as ineffective, since the padding absorbs a lot of force or pressure, and over -enthusiastic horses may only be made to see reason with difficulty. In principle this is right – however if you are reliant on a lungeing cavesson to control your horse, you should be giving

The German lungeing cavesson is distinguished by its thick padding, which can result in a less precise effect.

A lungeing cavesson made from leather with in-built loops for attaching the bit.

serious thought to the relationship you have with him. One real disadvantage which the German cavesson brings with it is its weight and size. It will more likely suit the coarser or larger horse's head. On an Arab's head, for example, it can be difficult to fit it correctly. In addition, such horses often feel uncomfortable, and show this by nodding their head or other expressons of displeasure.

Lungeing cavessons from France are in comparison much lighter. Styles range from a simple leather headpiece which is reinforced over the nose, to ones with an in-built jointed metal piece with attachments, which facilitates fitting, but can also concentrate the severity of its effect. In Spain the original form of the lungeing cavesson has been most closely retained. It consists of a half-rounded piece

Well suited for beginners: a French-style lightweight lungeing cavesson.

of metal, which is fitted to the shape of the nose. The severest type is the *serreta*, in which the metal is toothed. Translated, *serreta* means 'little saw', which describes the possible effect that the cavesson may have. Opinions are divided about the *serreta*: useful training aid or animal cruelty? Bleeding or scared noses, as a sign of a bad trainer, or immediate obedience and high-quality riding as a seal of quality for a good trainer? The *serreta* does not belong in the hands of a beginner; it may , if used at all, be used only by experienced professionals.

Regardless of the differences in the form that a lungeing cavesson may take, one requirement that they all must fulfill is that of being fitted exactly to the horse's nose. The prerequisite for good usage is a lungeing cavesson that sits well, does not slip but also does not hinder the horse's breathing in any way. The height that the noseband should be done up at (at least two fingerwidths above the corner of the mouth) should be considered, as well as the tightness. You should always be able to fit your thumb between the jaw bone and the leather. If it sits too high then it will press against the cheekbone, if too low then it will restrict breathing.

Ideally the lungeing cavesson should have an additional jaw strap that sits between the cheek and throat lash. This prevents the cheek pieces being pulled towards or into the eye. A throat lash is really superfluous apart from cosmetic effect. Three rings are attached to the noseband: the middle ring is for the leading rein (lunge rein), whilst the rings at either side are for the side reins.

The lungeing cavesson can also be combined with a bit, and offers an excellent opportunity

The jointed metal inlay in the French cavesson ensures that it can be fitted precisely.

to get a young horse gently used to the bit without hurting or damaging his sensitive mouth with (unintentionally) hard half-halts or hands.

As an optimal training aid for the beginner, you should always think of using the German lungeing cavesson in the first instance. Mistakes will be more easily for given, and unskilled use will have no great effect on the horse's sensitive nose. Nevertheless, its chief disadvantage may outweigh these advantages: a somewhat woolly transmission of the aids through the weight on the nose.

Considerably better models for beginners can be found amongst the French lungeing cavessons. A simpler, high-quality leather cavesson is considerably better to fit, forgives mistakes, but despite this also offers the trainer and the horse an insight into the way this piece of equipment should work. Jointed metal set into the noseband has the advantage that the cavesson can be fitted to many dif ferent

horses. Even horses that are particularly sensitive over the nose will willingly accept this type of lungeing cavesson.

Once you are experienced in the use of the lungeing cavesson, then you may wish to try out the original version with a smooth, iron nosepiece sewn into leather , without any increased severeness of course. Your aids will be transmitted directly – precisely and clearly.

Lungeing cavessons made out of synthetic materials are not to be recommended. They slip on the nose and are not to be compared with those made out of high-quality leather.

The bit

Whether loose ring or eggbutt snaffle, D ring or fulmer, single-jointed or double-jointed, thick or thin – the choice of bits is lar ge and there are virtually no limits to your

The lungeing cavesson proves itself on the lunge.

A JOINT DECISION

The choice between lunge cavesson or bridle should be made jointly with your horse – he will quickly show which he prefers. For horses with teeth or mouth problems, as well as those whose mouths have already been spoilt by previous riders, a well-fitted lunge cavesson can be a bitless alternative that has a precise effect. It works in many ways more relaxingly than a bit, and allows blockages and resistance to disappear much faster. There are however horses that can't bear pressure on their nose and feel confined by the nosepiece.

In these cases you can, with an easy conscience, chose a bridle instead. If you don't wish to give up on a bit totally when working with a lungeing cavesson, you can chose a combined cavesson. As required you can then do loosening work with the lungeing cavesson before moving on to working from the bridle.

If certain exercises aren' t successful after several attempts, then you should perhaps try the alternative option – often by doing this, the problem is solved.

The full cheek snaffle works on the outside of the mouth similar to a cavesson and stops the bit being pulled through the mouth.

imagination. There is only one thing that all these mouthpieces have in common – they are all a foreign body in the horse's mouth.

The gums, bars and tongue are all highly sensitive areas of the mouth, and a bit can cause a great deal of pain if it is used unknowledgeably and inappropriately. Unfortunately the knowledge of how a bit works and how to use bits is more often lacking, and leads to an of-

ten questionable use of these valuable means of communication.

Here too in-hand work has a great advantage over riding. You cannot tame a horse with force. As a trainer, you must look to the original mode of action of the bit: bending, flexing and limiting.

Whichever variation you decide on, correctly used, every bit can be a success. In practice, though, the full cheek snaffle has proven to be the best bit for use with in-hand work, since the bit ring cannot be pulled through the mouth if beginners make serious mistakes when starting out. The arms of the bit lie against the outside of the horse's mouth and have a similar effect to a cavesson. The corner of the mouth can't be pinched and the mouthpiece can't rotate on the tongue.

The whip

A further tool for in-hand work is that useful extension to the arm – the whip. Whips come in many lengths, strengths and designs. Ideally you should use a very light whip, since its use does require some experience. The heavier the whip, the tenser and more strenuous the work with the horse will become.

The length of the whip should be decided according to the demands and aims of the work and the sensitivity of the horse. It is important, though, that as an extension to your arm, it reaches to the horse's croup. In addition it must lie easily in the hand and allow for specifically aimed application, touching specific parts of the horse's body.

Praise

It is unusual to count praise as part of the basic equipment for in-hand work – it is however a very important factor in the development of a horse's training. Positive reinforcement when you have done something well contributes to understanding and to motivation, with humans as well as animals. Horses are very susceptible to praise. Clicker training has already used this fact to good effect and is based on the principle of asking, getting the correct answer, followed by praise.

This praise should follow immediately, so that the horse connects it to his correct answer. What reward you use is very much dependent on the individual horse. Often just words of praise suffice, a stroke over his body or a piece of carrot. More important is the genuineness of this reward. If you really aren't pleased and just say a brief 'Good', then it will not have the same effect as honest pleasure that comes from within. A carrot offered without emotion for the sake of it is really no praise, but rather a form of payment. A horse will recognise genuine joy and will react to passion with passion.

DO UNTO OTHERS …

... as you would have done unto you. Emotionless work, done without feeling and being obsessed with technique will result in a horse that acts in exactly the same way. By being honest, genuine and motivated in your work, a horse in return will work willingly alongside you.

Taking this into consideration, giving treats is not forbidden. This does assume that the horse is disciplined, accepts that you have your own personal space, and doesn't continuously demand further treats.

Starting out

The handler's position

The first steps in working in-hand should be made in a manege or indoor school. At the start, the outer boundaries of an indoor or outdoor school provide valuable help, and are often a necessity. The position shown in the pictures is the key to success during the initial phase. The horse should be on the outside track, the trainer on the inside track. The outside wall of the manege confines him on the outside, you, on the inside. Using the aids, the horse is thus framed on all sides.

The basic position for in-hand work on the horse's nearside
The handler should stand at the horse's shoulder, facing the horse. Your left hand holds the left rein, the right rein should be taken over the withers and held with the right hand, which also holds the whip.

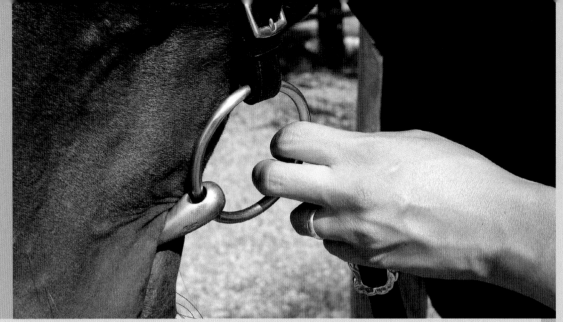

Option 1: Directly holding the bit.

Option 2: The hand holds the reins a few centimetres behind the bit.

Working from the bit

When starting out, the hand should hold the bit, producing a direct connection with the horse's mouth. A loose fist should be made, giving you every chance of giving the right aids and immediately feeling the horse's reaction from the mouth. In addition, the aids get

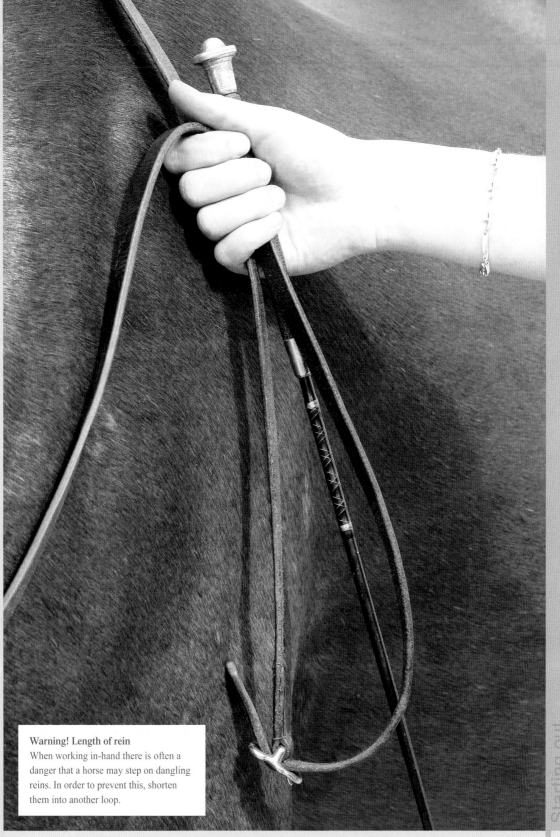

Warning! Length of rein
When working in-hand there is often a danger that a horse may step on dangling reins. In order to prevent this, shorten them into another loop.

to the horse directly and without the risk of interference. The contact needs to be quiet and it is then easy to follow the horse with your hands and lead him flexibly. In the case of a horse that tries to nip or snap at your fingers, this particular hold will automatically limit his chances of success. Alternatively you can hold the reins and create a contact with the horse's mouth. This second option should be chosen when using a lungeing cavesson or if he has a

longer neck which means that your arm's length does not enable you to take up the required position at his shoulder. In this position the hand controls the inner bit ring via the rein. You shouldn't forget that this longer distance to the mouth will have an effect on the precision and subtelty of the aids. The longer the distance between the mouth and the hand, the more irregular the contact can be. Using a lungeing cavesson causes no great problems,

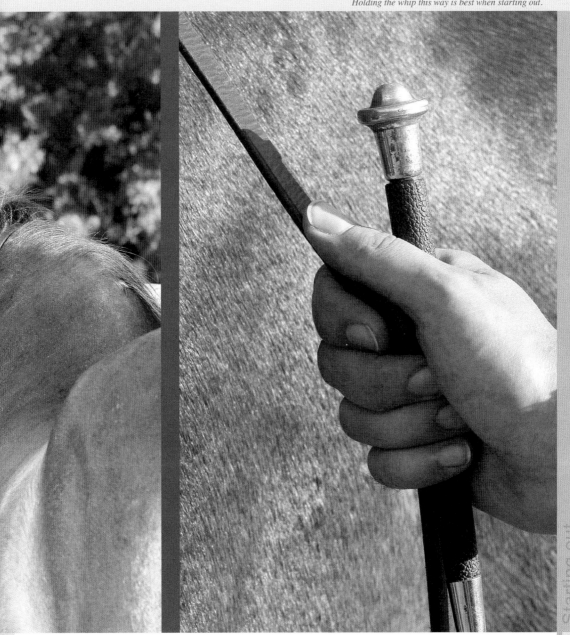

Holding the whip this way is best when starting out.

Open your hand, letting the outside rein lie across your fingers with the thumb on top.

The whip should be positioned between the thumb and first finger.

Close your fingers into a loose fist so you are holding the rein and whip in one hand under control.

indeed when working directly off the bit an unsteady hand may cause problems for more sensitive horses.

Holding the whip

Essentially there are two ways of holding a whip. The simplest way is to hold it with the rein, vertical to the ground. This is the best hold during the initial work, however for more advanced work such as lateral movements the second option should be used (see illustration).

Especially with in-hand work it is very important to be able to control your own body.

The whip needs to be used with precision and awareness in order to avoid any possible misunderstandings in communications with your horse. When working in-hand you can transmit the aids clearly and precisely to your partner the horse, and this is why at the start you should concentrate on ensuring that the aids are given clearly. A horse is very quickly overovertaxed, as are you. It is also important to observe the horse's own personal space. Your shouldn't stick to him like glue – keeping an appropriate distance between you and the horse is hugely important. The potential for problems increases if you pressurise the horse too much, causing him to stumble or get a fright.

The whip is pointed towards the hindquarters and can be used precisely.

Keep your distance! For reasons of safety and for the sake of his own personal space, you shold never stand too close to the horse.

A very common beginner's mistake is to stand too far forward, near to the horse's head. If you stand in front of his shoulder, you will constrain his forward movement, limit the field of vision and the space in front of the horse will be reduced. The horse will mostly fall behind the active aids and you won't have the horse 'in front' of you. With in-hand work you should never be leading, but always in a 'driving' position.

In addition you will only ever be able to bend the horse correctly when at the shoulder, something which is very important to all work done. It will probably take some time to get used to the correct position, however the path to lateral movements is blocked, in the true sense of the words, if you don't keep checking your position to the horse.

In the case of a lazy horse especially you may find yourself quickly too far forward after a few steps. If this is the case it is important not to get in front of his shoulder, so as to make it clear to him that he should go forwards energetically, and not trot behind you.

The aids

The influence of the hand is the most important aid for work done from the ground. In-hand work offers a rider the chance to clarify and explain the aids through the reins to the horse, step-by-step. One of the greatest advantages is that you are not sitting in the saddle transmitting your own tension through to the horse, which has its own consequences for the horse.

Of course, no leg aids can be given, so you have to seperate the effect of the hand from the legs: One after the other – hand without leg. This type of learning will be much easier for the horse and you will very quickly observe how sensitively the horse will react when the disrupting factor of a rider has been removed from his back.

If you look at the role of the hand in isolation, it is enormously important to understand what you are doing. If you are not aware of what you are doing, or don't know the function that the bit and the reins fulfill, then it will be impossible to transmit their purpose to the horse.

Initial basic exercises with the bit

Within the mouth, the bit can work on the tongue, the roof of the mouth (palate) and the bars of the mouth (the toothless area between the incisors and molars where the bit lies). These three areas are very sensitive to pain. If you pull back on both reins then in the case of a jointed snaffle it can pinch the tongue and press into the roof of the mouth. Unfortunately most horses have experienced this, whether it be in an exceptional situation ('Will you stand still!') or unfortunately also in the course of daily flat work ('I've got to get his head down!') Double-jointed or other more complicated mouthpieces can increase this nutcracker effect on the palate and will also have a similar effect on the tongue.

As a fundamental rule, therefore, the following should always be observed: both reins should never be taken up at the same time. In

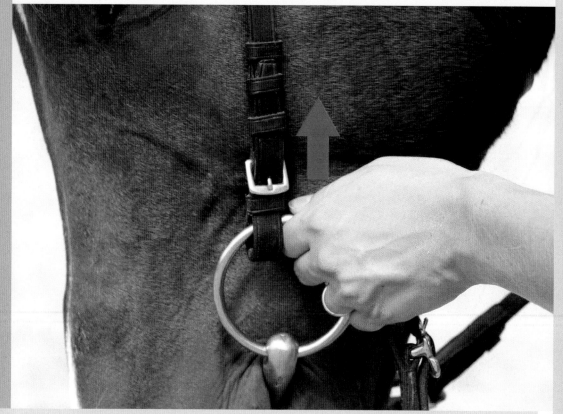

The hand moves towards the corner of the mouth, the roof and bars of the mouth are protected, and the tongue will not be pinched.

addition, the bit should always serve as an aid, never as a means of force or punishment. This rule applies just as much to riding as it does to working in-hand.

In the case of in-hand work especially, you should never be in a position to have to be rough with the reins. From the start you should always give well-directed and sensitive aids through the bit, the strength of the aid determined by the sensitivity of the horse: 'As little as possible, as much as necessary.' The reaction of the horse determines any further aids. Specifically, the hand works in three ways: upwards (lifting), sideways, or bending and lowering.

Lifting effect

Moving the bit towards the corner of the mouth causes the horse to lift his head, thus the entire forehand, supported by the effect of the hand, can be lifted. The poll and the height of the horse's head can be controlled. When you know what you want as a rider , then when working in-hand you have every opportunity to place the horse in the desired position.

Lowering effect

The downwards encouraging rein is unique to in-hand work. When riding, it is impossible to use the rein directly with a forwards-downwards effect – you would need metal poles,

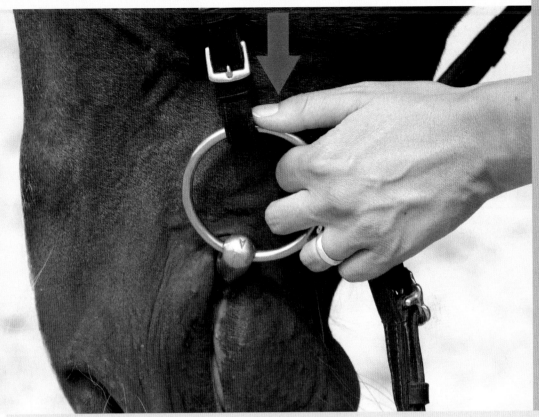

As the hand is lowered, the horse will try and avoid the pressure through his poll and lower his head.

rather than soft, flexible reins, to achieve this. If you are holding directly onto the bit, however, you are able to lead the bit down towards the ground, thus putting pressure on the horse's poll (similar to the effect of a double bridle), which causes the horse to give forwards and downwards and to follow the rein down.

Again and again in the riding world you encounter fanatics, who want only one thing from the horse: to go on the bit through the poll. The rest of the horse's movement and his balance are irrelevant; the main thing is that he is 'on the bit'. Many horses have incredible difficulties with this attitude. When hard hands try to force the horse to co-operate, then it is

hardly any wonder that the horse will go sour and will view work as a negative experience.

In order to achieve this lowering of the poll without having to play around too much with his mouth, you need to encourage the horse to lower. It is easy for the horse to give through his poll when his head is lower , since the movement required is so minimal that any horse will offer it.

However, in the case of horses with long, fine necks you must be very careful in encouraging the head to lower . The line from the horse's forehead down to his nose should not come behind the vertical, and you should avoid overbending, always paying attention that the

STRETCHING FOR NECK AND TOP LINE

The well-schooled horse follows (picture 1) the downwards encouraging rein, lowering his head, with the contact staying light but constant. The outside rein is given, without losing the contact. Your body language supports the horse in his movement and the horse will learn to always follow the direction of the rein, which can then be continued from the saddle.

In the second picture it is possible to clearly see the lowering tendency of the horse's head. The horse is beginning to bring his weight forward. There is a considerable weight in both the head and neck, and this moves the centre of gravity towards his shoulders. The muscles under his neck should relax and the entire topline will be stretched.

The lowering of his head will also cause the horse to relax. Horses that are excited will not lower their head. With the lowering rein you have a tool with whose help a horse can become both relaxed and balanced.

In the third picture the horse's topline is in the horizontal – for gymnastic exercises and for muscle stretching this is low enough. In the beginning it is all right for the horse to drop even lower, as long as his head doesn't tip behind the vertical. Correct exercises soon show the absurdity of overbending. By using in-hand work you can very quickly recognise overbending and correct it. Once the head is in a lower position you can bend the horse and complete the aid through the bit – from upwards through downwards into sideways. The lower the head, the easier it is to bend. Also, here it is a case of the horse's ears needing to stay at the same height. If they don't, then you as the handler need to look at the aids you are giving, most importantly the steady even contact on both reins.

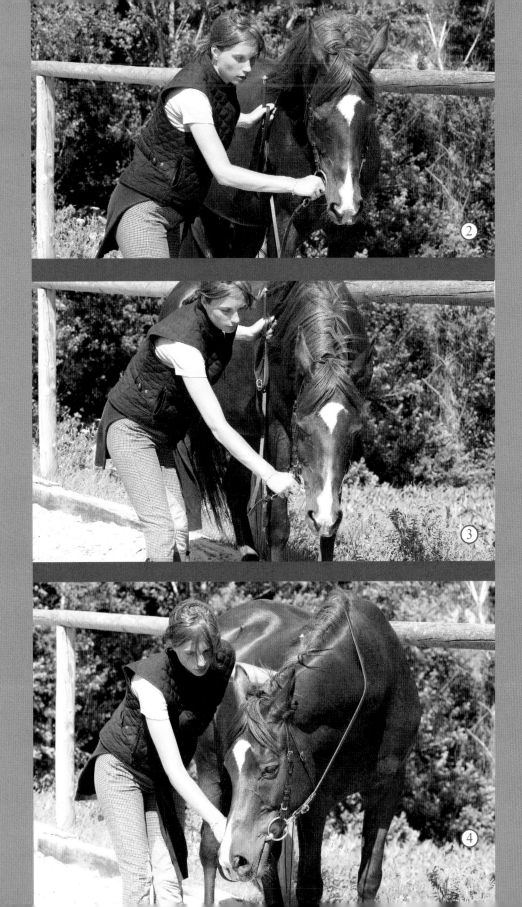

2

3

4

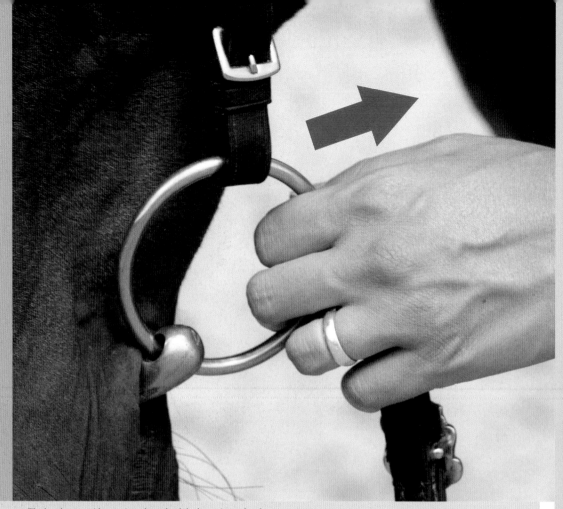

The hand moves sideways in order to lead the horse into a bend.

horse goes back to his normal position. Horses with long necks tend towards overbending, giving the impression of giving through the poll. When being ridden this tendancy can cause problems on its own and the horse will not then be truly on the aids and will not really be working on the bit. In-hand work can be very helpful with these cases as it is capable of showing the horse the correct position.

Bending effect

The third type of ef fect is the bending and flexing aid. Using the inside rein it is easy for the trainer to show and teach bending. Of course it is very important with in-hand work that in every instance and especially in the bend, there is a contact on both reins. The outside rein should follow and the inside should support. If you forget about the outside rein, which at the start is easy to do as you are moving independently of the horse, you may pull the bit through his mouth, causing him to tilt his head and react against the bit.As when riding, try and keep a steady contact through both reins. The outside rein which comes over the withers must for this reason always have a contact. Your hand should always feel the horse's offside.

THE INSIDE BEND

For the inside bend, here to the left, the inside, left hand makes a gentle upwards movement towards the corner of the horse's mouth, at the same time moving to the left. In the first photo this can be seen by the bit ring coming slightly away from the horse's head.

The outside, right rein stays in contact, but should not block the bend. You should 'feel' the outside rein, i.e. be in contact with his mouth. A gentle downwards movement of the right hand ensures this.

The trainer remains standing quietly in her position at the shoulder and is able to recognise how well the horse carries out the command. In the first photo the horse is positioned slightly to the left; in the second there is a lengthening and slight stretching which is complete in the third photo. The horse's ears stay at the same height – the horse is therefore not breaking through the poll. The position of his ears shows that he is paying attention and concentrating.

In the thrid photo it is also possible to see how well the outside rein is in contact against the horse's bent neck but does not restrict the bend. Using the sides of an arena or manege will prevent the horse's body moving and trying to avoid the bend, making the exercise much easier when starting out.

THE OUTSIDE BEND

In the case of the outside bend, here to the right, the left rein takes over the role of the outside, the right that of the inside rein. By moving the right hand down, towards the ground, the right rein will be tightened: the left hand helps by pressing gently against the horse's head.

In the first photo it is easy to see the counterposition, which becomes a counter bend in photo 2. The greater the outside bend the more the trainer's arm will be stretched; she should not move from her position, to avoid getting too far in front of the horse. The right rein bends and flexes the horse further, ensuring that the support through the left rein is not forgotten. In the third photo the maximum bend is

achieved and you will see that throughout this sequence the horse stays alert, relaxed and calm.

These exercises prepare the horse to bend away from the trainer, to move his shoulders and to undertake turns with a smaller radius than the trainer.

If you observe the trainer's position in the photos, you will clearly see that her left shoulder remains turned into the horse, but never gets so close as to put pressure on him, since the the horse is prepared to change where he is looking, to the right.

The muscles on the left side of his neck are stretched and those on the right-hand side are shortened – gymnastic exercises at a halt.

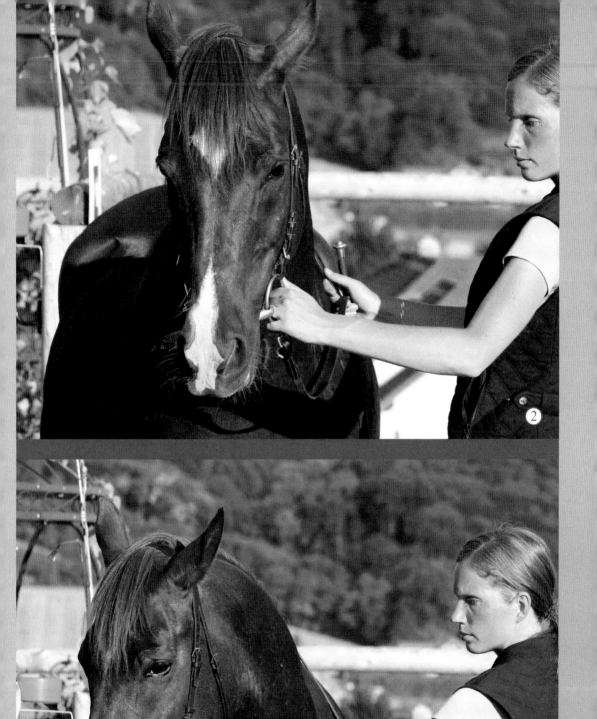

Initial basic exercises using the lungeing cavesson

The initial work using a lungeing cavesson differs in only a few details from the work with a bridle and bit. Bending and flexing here too are the main elements in this work. The lungeing cavesson is the ideal tool for all of the exercises shown in this book. Its greatest advantage is that it for gives human errors more readily than a bit. Thus the horse never has to suffer from the inexperience of his handler.

Fundamentally, as with working from the bit, half-halts through the cavesson have the same principle of giving and taking. When asking for bend, you do not just pull to the inside, but instead give the aid, bit by bit. The horse has to maintain the bend.

Basics of bending with a lungeing cavesson
The pressure of the rein (red arrow) produces pressure on the outside of the head to which the horse yields. This rein aid is understood by every horse. The right hand is on the neck in order to prevent any resistance.

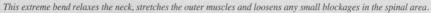

This extreme bend relaxes the neck, stretches the outer muscles and loosens any small blockages in the spinal area.

Towards the ground

In a lungeing cavesson a horse must also learn to stretch downwards at a halt.
The rein shows the way with your body accompanying it.

Outside bend

In order to improve the angle, and through this the effect of the rein on the cavesson,
you should lift your hand slightly (blue arrow) to create the bend.

The horse in movement

The favourite side

In the initial work done at a halt you will have found a mutual language, the horse has become accustomed to the rein aids and has learned, to relax through stretching and bending and the lowering of his neck. In addition, through this work you will get a feel for which side the horse finds it harder to bend through. Just as you have a good and a bad side, so your horse will have one side on which he finds the work easier. Throughout the training process you will be reminded again and again of this one-sidedness. Despite this, it is one of the most important things to ensure that both sides of your horse are evenly worked. Gradually you will become more experienced and skilled in co-ordinating the bit and whip, and when you attempt the advanced exercises you should not find them too difficult.

In these first exercises in walk, dealing with both will pose a great challenge. You will be used to leading from the left, saddling from the left and mounting from the left. In the case of in-hand work, you will need to work from the right-hand side as well. This is unusual not only for you; horses often find this strange as well – the effort will be greater than on the familar right-hand side.

After a few sessions when a new routine becomes established, any tension will start to dissolve and working from both sides of the horse should cause no great problems.

Less is more

In-hand work is no replacement for simple therapeutic exercise. All exercises are specially developed gymastic exercises, which will often bring a horse to the limits of his physical capabilities.

'Every journey starts with the first step' is a well-known saying. This first step has been made with the work done at a halt. All the following exercises need to be worked through and approached just as carefully.

You should not over-estimate your horse's attention span. Targeted learning demands a high level of attention, and is real 'brain work'. The horse needs to think along with you, and has to actively participate. If the horse becomes psychologically tired and lets himself becomes distracted, he needs a break. During this break he can process what he has been learning. In-hand work is not just physical work but also mental work.

Also important is that clear guidelines and clear aids will enable a horse to feel better about himself. Through the understanding that is demanded, most horses develop a true enjoyment of their work. The responding praise from the trainer at the right time increases the motivation and ambition of the horse enormously, and all movements will become easier as a result. With time, the horse will respond with greater sensitivity and attention to the trainer, because he has learnt to pay attention. On this foundation he will be able to approach the harder exercises with more ease and complete them successfully faster.

Clear rules for leading and moving forwards

Most problems start to emerge with leading and when asking the horse to move forwards. In their natural state in a herd, the dominant mare takes over the lead. She goes at the front of the herd, with the rest following her. The dominant stallion drives the herd and controls it by setting a pace of his own choosing from behind.

With in-hand work you are located at the horse's shoulder – in principle too far behind his head to lead him in what would be considered a correct way, and too far forward to drive him forwards from the rear. In a herd, foals take up this position next to their mother or close friends that they are growing up with. As his trainer, though, you want to lead, steer and drive your horse from this position. That is why it is enormously important that the horse understands this and accepts and respects your proximity, which in the case of in-hand work is close.

Your body language must be clear and concise, otherwise misunderstandings will occur. Not only, but especially, in the case of in-hand work, clear rules need to be laid down between horse and handler. When you are standing next to your horse you are within easy reach of his entire body. Running away, threatening or biting are not acceptable forms of behaviour – on the one hand, assertiveness and consistency is required of the trainer and on the other hand discipline on the part of the horse. Mutual respect should also not be forgotten.

In daily dealings, whether when grooming, saddling or leading, a horse has to know exactly what he can and cannot do. The same is the case when working in-hand. Clear rules makes progress easier and allow for quicker comprehension. In this case, the horse has to understand that when you are at his shoulder, you are neither a foal nor a playmate to be bitten or threatened.

The walk as the foundation

The most comfortable pace for the work described here is the walk. It is the slowest of all the paces and therefore best suited for starting out, since the trainer will not have the same condition and fitness as the horse, and is unlikely to be able to keep up with a horse's ground-covering trot for long.

Despite this, the horse is hardly likely to get bored – the exercises are varied, and will give the horse plenty to think about. With continued training, not only will the ability of the horse be improved, but also the fitness of the trainer. Thus, in-hand work is not only an enrichment for your four-legged friend, but also has health and fitness benefits for you.

The horse's balance and ability to carry himself will quickly be improved and will enable him to increase his ability to collect. At this stage nothing will stand in the way of working at a trot. Correctly carried out lateral movements also bring the horse a bit closer to carrying more weight through his hocks and hindquarters, and as a result to greater awareness of his own body and better movement.

Walk on

The aids for moving forward when working in hand comprise the following:
• tension in the body
• position of the body
• voice
• whip.

Incorrect: The trainer is too far forward and is blocking the forward movement.

The first two points are of the greatest importance. From the basic position we have already dealt with, you will need to create a positive tension in your body and bring yourself to attention before turning in the direction of the desired movement. Lean forward when starting to take the first step. If the horse does not react, use an encouraging voice aid (e.g. 'Walk on!'). Only if he still doesn't walk off should you resort to a light touch of the whip – first at the girth, then at the side of his croup. Every horse reacts differently to the whip, therefore you will need to experiment with what is the required force.

You should only use the whip until the horse reacts. A lazy horse will need to be woken up rather more than a nervous one. Moving the whip to create a sound in the air may be more effective than just touching him. However you do it: as soon as you get a reaction – in this case walking forward – you must stop the aid. Only thus will a horse respond lightly to the aids and not be dead to the aid. Never lose sight of the goal – the willingness to move forward as a result of the aids from your body.

A frequent reason why a horse doesn't step forward is often that the way forward is blocked. Often you will find yourself too far in front of the horse without noticing. At the first step from a standstill, your body must still be next to the horse's shoulder. If you use the aids for moving forward but stand in his way at the same time, then the aids will not be clear and the horse may become stressed.

IMPORTANT: THE POSITION OF THE BODY

In the photos you can clearly see how important the position of your body is. Just before moving off the trainer turns slightly in the direction of the movement. (Photo 1)

Now comes the first step: the right wrist holding the whip turns so that the whip comes into a position from which it may be used. If the horse doesn't move off with you, then it can be used if necessary at the girth. Particular attention should be given to the correct position here too. The horse should step forward with the trainer and not fall behind. The horse's head must stay in front of the trainer's body. The trainer's left shoulder should turn away from the horse, thus making the way clear. The preparation for halting can

be seen in the third photo. The trainer moves her upper body slightly back, turns towards the horse again and stands still.

Normally no pressure will be taken up on the rein, in fact quite the opposite. At the start you should give with both the inside and outside rein. The horse should react to the turning of your body and your own halt, not to any backwards pressure from the rein.

In the fourth photo you can see that the horse has opened up slightly through his neck and come slightly in front of the vertical.

The basic rule should always be: if the trainer moves, then the horse should move. If the trainer stands still, then so should the horse.

④

Halt

Stopping is easy – or is it? In theory, halting a horse shouldn't be a problem. You stop and stand your horse when handling him all the time: before opening the gate to his field, when grooming or saddling. Despite this, you see so many that are being towed around behind their horse, when they should be the ones in the lead. Many riders resort to a bit in order to keep their horse, at least for some of the time, under control.

With in-hand work however, the aid to halt has a great significance. If you are sitting on your horse and he doesn't halt when asked, then it just takes a few metres more to come to a halt. When you are beside him on the ground however then it isn't quite so straightforward. Horses by their very nature are stronger and faster than us, and taking a few metres more to stop might mean that your arm is wrenched painfully, or you are towed along after him. For this reason, being able to ensure your horse halts consistently when asked is very important, and you should use every aid available to ensure you can do this.

This is why you should also use your voice as an aid for the halt. Regardless of whether you say 'Halt' or 'Stand', what is important is that the tone used is always the same, and that praise immediately follows any positive reaction. Especially at the beginning, it is good to have as wide a selection of aids at your disposal as possible – it is then all the easier to achieve what you want. If your voice, supported by your own body, is sufficient to get the required halt, then you don't need to give any further aids. This constitutes a well-known principle of all equine eduction: use as much as necessary, and as little as possible!

The greatest advantage of in-hand works lies in the fact that you aren't on the horse's back. If you were sitting in the saddle and your horse decides to keep going, then you are forced to go along as well. When working in-hand though, you can stay where you are, independent of your horse. This is a hugely important aid, which makes it very clear to the horse what is expected of him.

Applying the aids using a lungeing cavesson

The command for halting when using a lungeing cavesson is different from that when using a bit, in several respects. Pulling on both reins is to be avoided just as it is with the bit. The resulting backwards-working pressure opens the way for a counter resistance. This is why it is especially important when applying the aid to be very aware of your body language. Any aid or half-halt applied to the cavesson needs to be given as if you were vibrating the rein, or as if ringing a bell – quickly alternating between taking and giving.

Problem: the horse won't stop

The most common cause of a horse not responding to the aid to halt is stress. Uncontrolled pulling on the reins causes pain to the mouth; the whip is usually, unwittingly, kept in a position to drive the horse on, whilst the horse is blocked from being able to move on. All of these can result in tension, that prevents the horse from being able to halt quietly and in a relaxed manner.

Detailed aids for the halt with a lungeing cavesson
The red arrows mark your aids. Your outer shoulder should turn towards the horse, your hip tips slightly back and allows your leg and upper thigh to lock into the halt. Your upper body should go slightly behind the vertical in order to emphasise and reinforce your body's message. The whip should be pointed downwards, in a passive position. The inner rein may be used to give a halt-halt if necessary, remembering to hold onto the outside rein without giving, so that the horse doesn't turn in by mistake.

The aids for halt are:
- tension through the body
- voice
- the position of the body in relation to the horse
- use of the reins.

To halt, you should breathe out to relax the body, quietly give the command to halt, turn your body in towards the horse and give through the reins. The whip must be lowered and lie loosely in the hand. Don't forget to give praise when the halt is achieved.

Another possible cause of disobedience to the aid to halt is that the horse simply ignores you and has decided to keep going. In this instance it is necessary to move your body in front of your horse slightly, in addition to using your voice. The fourth element in the aid to halt can now be used together with an upwards pressure on the bit (see picture on

Here the whip is still in a driving position. The horse reacts to this and doesn't come to a halt immediately.

If a horse consistently refuses to halt, then taking hold of the bit itself should be the last resort. An upwards half-halt will have even the most stubborn of horses responding. It should be used sparingly, though. The next time, the other aids should used, if at all possible, in preference.

page 60. In this way, you are collecting the horse up and transferring his centre of gravity backwards. Due to this changed balance he should have no option but to halt.

Under no circumstances should you lower the hand holding the reins, nor let them move back. This only encourages the horse to start a tug of war with you. A horse halted in this way will usually fall behind the vertical and is trained to go against the bit – something which is counterproductive for the training process.

Caution is also needed if you relinquish your position at the horse's shoulder to move into a more forward position. In these circumstances, keeping a safe distance at the side of the horse is important to avoid being run over.

Learning the halt is enormously important in the horse's eduction. Without the halt, there can be no riding. Unfortunately, less and less value is placed on achieving a correct and consistent halt, which often leads to the mouth being pulled on again and again. In-hand work is an excellent way of teaching a calm, stress-free and consistent halt from the start.

STRENGTH LIES IN PATIENCE

Horses are quite happy to stand still for hours in the field. Stress in their relationships with people often causes this natural behaviour to disappear. When grooming, a horse may not stand still, between the field and stable it is pointless to even think about stopping, and when riding he won't stand still for even a second.

Why is this? First and foremost, it is we who are responsible. In a world that is governed by hectic schedules and time management, a pause appears to bring with it only disadvantages. To achieve a consistent halt you require above all calm and patience.

Don't let the moment be disrupted by clock-watching or allowing thoughts of your work or private responsibilities to cause stress. Only then can you and your horse ensure a mental balance also at a halt.

Strong aids through the rein can also be counterproductive for quietly standing still. Pain to the mouth causes stress, and stress will arouse the flight instinct.

There are some horses that try to run away, and others who face and fight danger by rearing. Everyone will recognise the picture of rider and horse fighting each without an apparent winner. This is a real shame, as by utilising in-hand exercises it is possible to create and refine the foundations of a good halt.

The forward position at his head, turning your entire body towards him and the half-halt on the inside rein should all combine to ensure your horse will step back.

The horse transfers his weight back and steps back with diagonal legs. Using the outside track should stop the reinback going crooked when beginning.

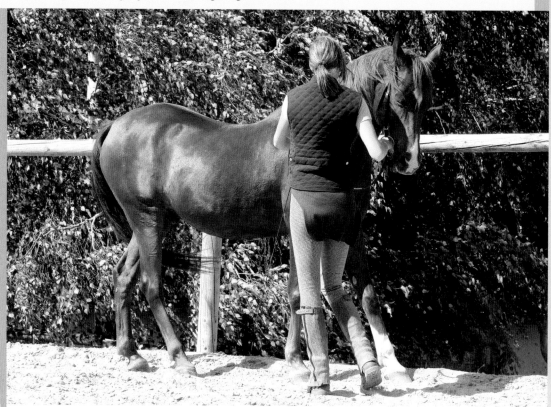

Rein-back

After the walk and the halt, there is another basic lesson that any horse must learn: the rein-back. This lesson can also be taught in-hand, often much better and faster than when riding, thanks to the possibilities offered by body language.

Step-by-step instructions for this are as follows:

- The trainer's position gives her horse the first instruction. You should stand slightly in front and closer to the horse's head, and thus block his field of vision. In the initial attempts you may stand at an angle in front of him in order to emphasise the effect of your own body. You should never stand directly in front of the horse, due to the risk of being walked over if he should be startled or take fright.
- Your voice command should be a slow and drawn out 'Ba-ack', which underlines your intention and will train him to this command.
- Slowly but surely step towards the horse, at the same time giving a gentle half-halt on the inside bit ring. Accompanied by the voice command the horse should step back. If he doesn't then, to support the aids, you can put your hand on his chest and use as much pressure as neccesary to underline your body language.

In the case of attentive and hard-working horses, your own body language should suffice, but in the case of lazy or stubborn horses you may need more help to start with. But here too it is a case of as soon as the horse takes a step back, stop asking and offer praise. Next time, you should be able to reduce the amount asked in order to give the horse the chance to react to a more subtle aid.

When the horse is more practised, then a slight turn of your upper body and the voice command should suffice to send him back. Your basic position at the horse's shoulder should then not need to be sacrificed.

In order to keep the horse straight, begin the lesson on the outside track. If his croup should start to turn to the inside, then it should be enough to turn his neck slightly to the inside during the rein-back.

Routine and experience

When beginning the first steps of in-hand work it is essentially a matter of the horse:

- going forwards with the trainer in response to the aids
- staying in position with his trainer
- not being pushy or pressing
- standing still when the trainer stands
- not getting excited or upset and getting used to the work.

All these points should be practised and achieved before getting the horse used to staying next to you at any chosen place in the manege. In the case of schooling patterns, you shouldn't worry too much about getting the correct bend. More important is that the horse stays in the same position in relation to his trainer.

On curves, you will mostly be on the inside and be able to pay more attention to both your own and the horse's position. The precision

In this turn to the right the horse is bent away from his trainer, to the right. The left rein functions as the outer rein, the right rein takes over as the inside rein. As with flexing at a standstill, the left hand can help to bring his head to the right.

In this picture it is easy to see how the horse is bent and flexed by his trainer. The horse is paying attention and is learning that he doesn't always have to be bent around his handler. The right, inside rein is giving the required degree of bend for the circle. The left hand is helping the horse with the bend, and is supporting the right rein.

of the aids will gradually become more important.

A horse that has a tendency to go too fast can be persuaded to go at a slower pace on a circle, since you can keep up with him, having a smaller distance to walk yourself, without the need for running.

If, after changing the rein, you end up on the outside, your own position will be slightly more forward because the horse must stretch his outside (the side towards you), and this will get longer. Due to the length of your arms which have a limited reach, it means you will be stepping slightly in front of the horse.

Schooling figures explained

Circles, ten- and six-metre circles (voltes), serpentines etc are vital for working in-hand. It is not a matter of chasing him from one figure to the next, but giving him the required balance so that he can work around the manege in a supple manner. You will also benefit hugely from this work when riding.

A significant advantage of in-hand work is that you can carry out the school figures very precisely because you just have to do them correctly yourself. If you make a correctly rounded circle then your horse will do the same, if you make the circle smaller then you

INSIDE AND OUTSIDE

The same definition applies as with riding: the inside is always on the 'hollow' side of the horse. If the horse is turned and bent to the left, then the left-hand side of the horse is his inside.

If the horse is going absolutely straight, then there is no inside or outside. As a point of reference, though, you would take the middle of the arena as the inside.

In the case of work done in-hand you wouldn't always be to the inside, but might also be to the outside. The horse isn't always going to bend around you, but will also bend away from you.

will soon end up doing a volte. The direction is easily determined; as trainer you are better able to concentrate on achieving the correct bends and turns necessary for building-up flexibility and muscle development.

Going large

The horse should be on the outside track, the trainer on the inside track. On the long side the horse should be straight, but when going large he needs to go deep into the corners. The bend in the corners is made easier, thanks to

Going large

the outside edge of the manege that underpins and can replace the outside, supporting aids. The preparation for the bend is important. Before reaching the corner the horse should be bent to the inside in order to complete an accurate bend.

After the corner the horse should be straightened using the inside hand and the outside rein.

When working in-hand, this school figure is little used, since it is a long distance to cover on foot and it is more like leading the horse out for a walk than a true suppling exercise.

Circles

The first 'real' school figure is the circle. The arc described by a 20-metre diameter circle is

Circle

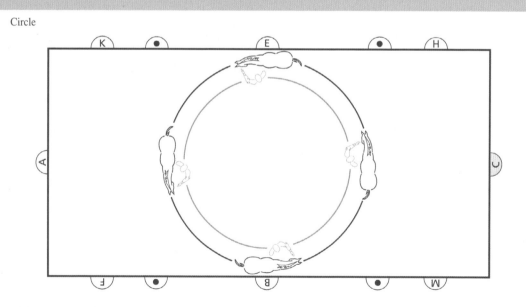

Volte

ideal for teaching a horse bend and flexion. The degree of bend made is relatively small. The neck must however be positioned to the inside in order to achieve the correct latitudinal bend. The handler herself should make a smaller circle to the inside, so that the horse walks faster than she does.

The circle can be undertaken in the middle of the manege (see illustration) or can begin at A or C. In the latter two cases the corners are of course rounded, with the horse on the outside track only briefly.

Volte – ten-metre circles and smaller

What the circle is to a young horse, is a volte to a more advanced horse. This small circle with initially a ten-metre diameter, later much smaller, demands a much greater flexibility and suppleness. With in-hand work it is possible to very soon work on smaller circles in order to recognise and overcome the problems that the horse has, due to his natural one-sidedness

Also on the volte, the horse's bend needs to follow through the arc made by the circle.

This is only possible with the necessary preparatory suppling exercises – otherwise the already crooked horse will try to evade the need to bend by swinging his quarters, falling out through his shoulder or falling in on the inside.

Single- and double-loop serpentines

Single- and double-loop serpentines consist of a series of parts of different-sized circles. In a single-loop serpentine the bend through the first corner is greater, followed by a stretch of straightness, then a lesser bend on the other rein and then another deeper bend in the second corner.

For the trainer this figure consists of a volte, then you position the horse for the middle bend as if on a circle moving away from you, followed by a straightening before leading again into a volte (refer to the description given for changing the rein on page 70). The single- or double-loop serpentine is an excellent exercise for practising changing the bend when working in-hand. The aids change twice and the outer edge of the manege helps

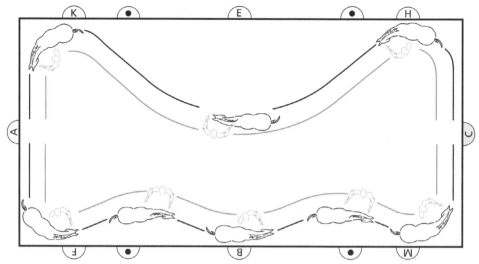

Single- and double-loop serpentines

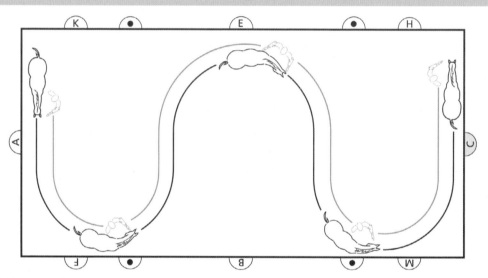

Triple-loop serpentine

Square circle and square volte.

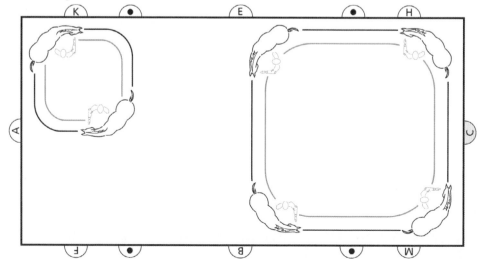

with the volte parts of the figure, so that despite the degree of bend required, the horse doesn't fall out through the shoulder or quarters.

Triple-loop serpentines

Carrying on from the single-loop serpentine, the triple-loop version across the width of the school so that each loop touches the long side of the arena, offers the advanced horse much more variation and opportunity for practising transitions of pace, combinations of lateral movements, or the two together.

In principle there is no difference to the single-loop serpentine. The middle loop is more demanding for the handler, since he has to describe a half-volte on the outside of the horse and must precisely control both the balance and the speed of the horse throughout. For the horse, every loop must be the same size, but for the trainer, their size will depend on her position in relation to the inside or outside.

20-metre square circles

This school figure is a very important one for in-hand work. The actual length of the figure is not too long, the support from the outside edge of the manege is present for two corners and the required bend is demanding.

It is in effect a square circle, its equivalent for advanced horses being a square volte. In the latter the corners are carried out as a quarter-pirouette, which is particularly useful for suppling the horse. Combined with lateral movements, this exercise is extremely useful and is fun for both horse and handler.

The centre line

This school figure follows the centre line and for in-hand work is more an exercise used to check whether the horse stays straight without the help of the outside edge of the manege. The outer rein and the position of the handler are very important here in ensuring that the horse does not fall out through the quarters. You, as

The centre line

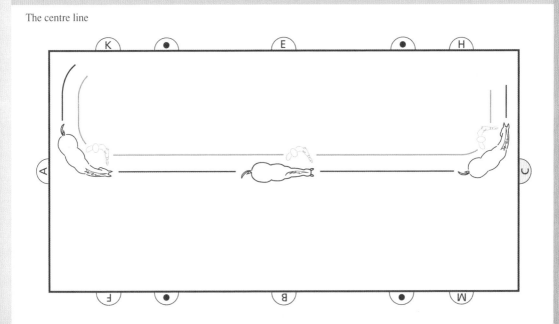

the trainer, need to be very focused on the end points at A or C: only then will a horse carry out the exercise successfully without the assistance of an outside permanent barrier.

Different options
for changing the rein

Unlike long reining, where the handler changes sides following a change of hand, the handler remains on the nearside when changing rein. A change of rein means that the handler proceeds on the outside track and the horse on the inside track. With straight lines, in principle nothing changes – although many horses will try to move over to the outside track. This pushing of the trainer further to the outside is in most cases an indication of a lack of respect, and at the first sign must be coun-

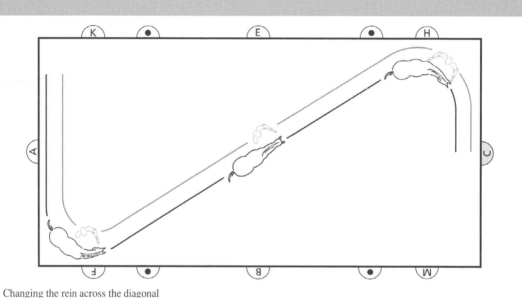

Changing the rein across the diagonal

Changing the rein diagonally across half the school

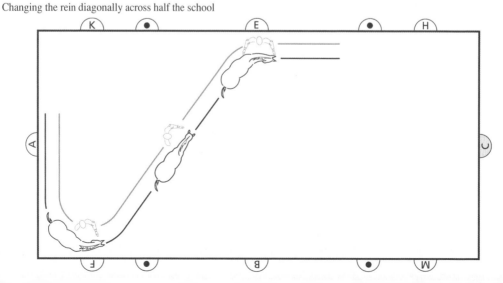

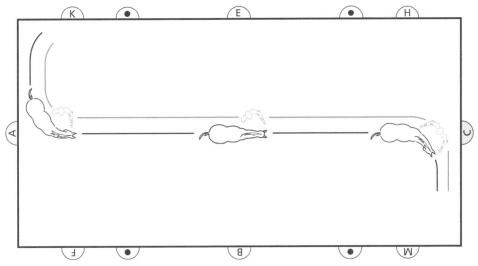

Changing the rein down the centre line

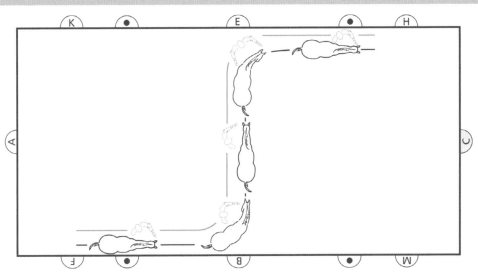

Changing the rein across the middle of the school at B or E

Changing of rein from circle to circle

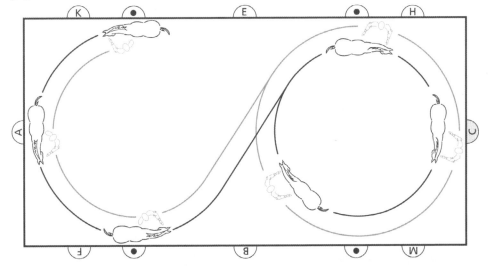

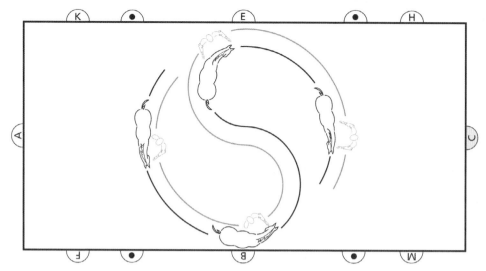

Changing through the circle

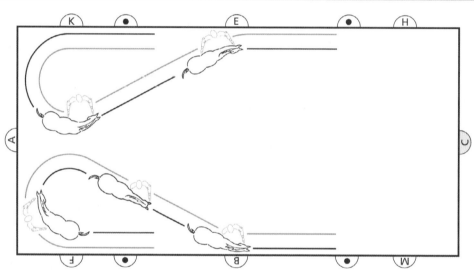

Half-circle out of the corner with a change of rein

Half-circle into the corner with a change of rein

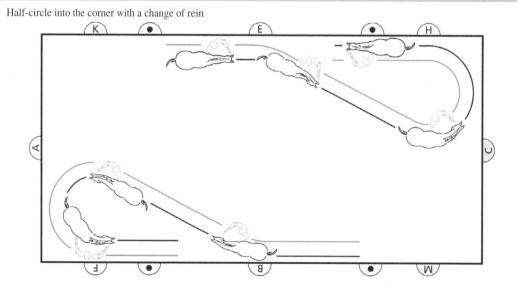

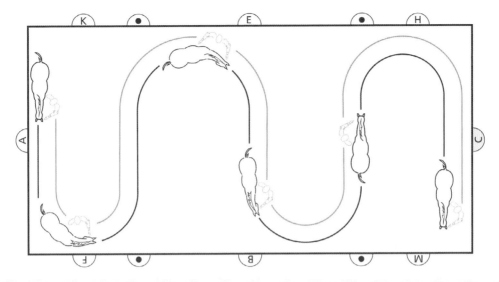

Serpentine with four loops, each touching the track. It should be recognised that the loops are different sizes for the handler but not for the horse.

tered by assuming a consistently straight and self-confident bearing yourself, whilst remaining pointedly on the desired track. Should the horse continue to press to the outside, then you should use an outstretched inside arm to keep the horse at the required distance. As a last resort you should tap the horse on his shoulder with the whip, to show him that there are boundaries that must not be crossed.

Since the horse on the inside track will be drawn automatically to the outside, there is a further difficulty in keeping him straight. When practising lateral movements this can be helpful, however when going in a straight line this must be avoided. Exact and consistent control over both the position of the handler's body and the reins are decisive factors.

When bending, the horse may be bent away from his handler. In addition the horse will be walking a shorter distance than his handler, who for this reason must move faster than when she is to the inside. When placed to the outside, what was formerly the inside rein becomes the new outside rein, and vice versa. The whip is now located on the side of the horse that is stretched and the handler should

be able to confine her horse from the outside.

Opportunities for changing the rein are endless. Classical dressage has a number of suitable school movements, although the principle is always the same, so that they offer the same challenges for both horse and trainer undertaking in-hand work.

Flexion, bend, going forwards

It is now time to balance the horse so that he is able to achieve self-carriage. Being balanced in his movement means that as a trainer, you put the horse into an outline and position that enables him to work correctly on a circle. It is important to maintain the suppleness and relaxed movement achieved throughout the initial work. From now on the horse should always show correct flexion and bend, for without bend, in principle he will not be able to turn – a horse that is supple must be able to find his balance not only on straight lines, but also on wide and narrow turns. Once the horse understands that his new outline and position does him good and helps him in his work,

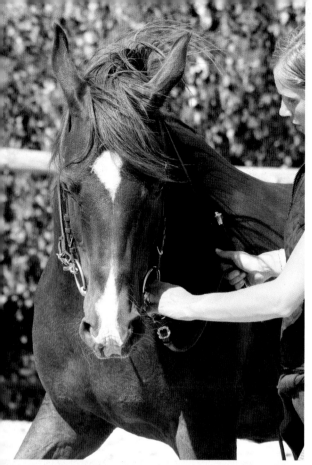

On the circle this horse is correctly flexed and bent, reacts to light aids and is in self-carriage. Supple and alert, he is ready for advanced work.

this basic work, then he will find it relatively easy to master the harder exercises. Lateral movements – a closed book for many – will, thanks to the preparation undertaken, become an exercise that is both understood and physically possible for the horse.

On the circle

As soon as the horse has been familiarised with the schooling figures and is easy to lead and teach, work on the circle can begin. A lowered head is the first aim, as in this position the neck can be much more easily bent and flexed – the muscles on the underside of the neck are more relaxed and won't offer as much resistance to the hand.

Start on the circle at E or B, and start with the downwards encouraging rein (see page 43). Once moving forward, most horses do not find it difficult to respond to this aid. Once the head is lowered, the inside hand gives small half-halts to place the horse's head to the side and the horse will then start to turn around the trainer.

In this phase of training it is hugely important that the handler continues to stay consistently on her own circle line, doesn't allow the horse to push her out of her position, and doesn't get in front of the horse's movement. This can be difficult when dealing with an inexperienced or stiff horse.

Often, horses may fall slightly onto the inside shoulder, placing their weight to the inside, bend to the outside and thus cause the circle to become smaller. To counter this, you should stroke or touch the neck on the near side, as was done when stationary, massaging it if necessary. Nothing is achieved at this stage

allowing him to respond to the aids with more lightness and sensitivity, then the door will be wide open for lateral movements. All you need to do is walk through it.

The Portugese schoolmaster, Nuno Oliveira, developed a wonderful training moto that sums up a horse's entire course of training: 'Prepare, and then let it happen.' This is a good way of expressing the way in which a horse should always be balanced so that he finds it easy to carry out an exercise or a movement by himself. Bending both when stationary and when moving is the preparation for all further lessons. If a horse is relaxed and supple in

The aids through the rein that encourages the horse to take the rein down puts him in a position that allows him to bend more easily…

…and to find his own balance.

The horse in movement

A hand on the neck can sometime work wonders.

by pulling on the inside rein. The horse will simply fight the pressure on the bit and continue to put his weight on the inside shoulder.

The half-halts on the inside rein are therefore supported by a hand on the neck. Only when working in-hand do you have this invaluable aid at your disposal. What the inside leg does when riding can be achieved much more easily, and (for the horse) more understandably, by the hand.

Fundamentally, a horse with a long, high-set neck will not find flexion as difficult as a stockier horse with a short, thick neck. These factors will also determine how long the exercises can be carried out for. The harder it is to bend through the neck or to position the horse's head to the inside, the longer you will need to persist with this exercise.

In the case of horses with short necks in particular, it is easy for them to lift the head and tense the neck muscles. As a result, the steps taken will be far too short, he will set his neck and the horse's body cannot be moulded. In these cases the bend will need to be reduced and the horse encouraged to lower his head again, ensuring that the horse continues to move forward energetically. As a result the quarters should step well underneath his body.

Giving with the rein is, and remains, one of the most important elements of this exercise. The aim is for the horse to maintain the flexion by himself, without need of the bit, and for you to only feel the weight of the rein in your hand.

What is the correct bend?
In the case of work on circles, many trainers experience great concern about the horse falling out through the outside shoulder, but greater concern that there is too much bend. As already shown in the work when at halt, you should not be afraid of too much bend. When working on the circle the horse can be bent to a great degree.

When working in-hand, it is rare for a horse to run out through his shoulder, since just by stopping, the trainer can prevent this at any time. The horse will quickly realise that his handler does not have to go with him when he tries to evade, since she is not seated in the saddle but rather can remain where she is on the circle. The rein can be used not only to restrict but also of course to stop the horse. As soon as the limit of the combined distance of the trainer's arm and the outside rein is reached, the horse will learn to recognise and accept the limitation to his movement. Only in the case of very large or long horses is it necessary sometimes to ask for a greater degree of bend to exert added control of the shoulders. It is especially helpful to use the exercise on a circle whereby the circle is made smaller and then larger, ensuring that the flexion and bend is controlled throughout, and the reaction to the outside bend is also checked constantly.

If the horse does fall out with this quarters, you need only to move towards the forehand and increase the tempo – there is no supporting outside leg as there would be when riding. You enlarge the circle through the forehand and utilise the driving aid, otherwise the horse is likely to fall out further through the quarters.

By pushing the shoulders more to the outside, you are causing the circle to become larger than intended. Keeping to an exact-sized circle only becomes important later on in

Here the quarters are threatening to fall out.

By directing the shoulders more to the outside ...

... the horse's centre of gravity is changed.

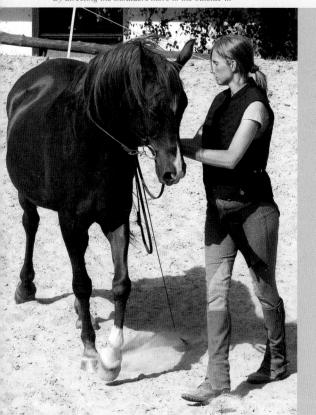

training. As long as you don't lose control over the forehand and quarters, the symmetry of the circle is less important. Most significant is maintaining the control of the horse's forehand – this will become increasingly important throughout the training.

Common handler errors

One of the most frequent mistakes is 'sticking' to the horse. If you stand too close, correct application of the aids will be impossible. The whip will be ineffective as a driving aid, and the personal space of both horse and trainer will be infringed.

From this position you will lose sight of the entire horse, only seeing the neck, and be unable to form a picture of the whole horse. Again, this will be more important for the exercises to come.

An additional mistake is in keeping an incorrect position in relation to the horse. Very often the trainer is too far in front of the horse – thus blocking the horse's field of vision and acting as an optical brake.

The direction of the inside arm should serve as a reference point – if it is angled too much, then usually the position is wrong.

Also needing correction is the frequent tendency to pull the inner bit ring to the inside. The outside rein is no longer just on a light contact, and the bit itself is pulled through the mouth. In reaction to this the horse will tip his head. His ears will no longer be level and the muzzle will be closer to the trainer than his poll. The outside rein must be matched with the same degree of pressure as on the inside rein, and remain in contact. The inside hand must always give and limit any risk of pulling.

Too close to the horse
This risks losing the horse's respect. In addition the whip is useless from this position, because you are not able to properly use it. The arms are too bent and can maintain no distance.

Here the position is correct
The left arm is extended slightly, the ouside rein can establish a soft contact to the bit, and the appropriate distance to maintain respect has been established.

Here the handler is too far forward: her left arm is too bent, causing the right arm to be too extended.

Much better: the position at the shoulder with the inner arm extended.

The reaction of pulling on the inside rein: the horse tips his head.

The aids when using a lungeing cavesson

At this stage of training the lungeing cavesson shows its real utility. Due to its direct effect on the bend you have a tool that can work wonders.

In the case of the lungeing cavesson, as opposed to the bridle, there is no 'mental brake' – the horse knows that he can't be pulled in the mouth. Reprimands given via the nasal bone don't lack effect, but are perhaps a more understandable punishment for the horse to which he can react quickly.

Without this brake, lazy horses are often more prepared to co-operate, and only by going forwards is it possible for a proper bend to occur.

The aids need to be given in exactly the same way as when working off a bit. A lungeing cavesson can only have a turning effect when the inside hand is kept low. If the half-halt is given too high, then the angle of the rings on the cavesson is changed and the effect is reduced considerably. The heightened angle causes the noseband to be pulled up the nose and can cause rubbing. For this reason it is very important that the inside hand is kept low and any commands are given from that position.

As a result of the leading hand being in the correct position, the horse will be easy to flex and to bend. Also when in a cavesson, it is important that the horse's head doesn't get too high and that he moves actively with his handler. Any corrections should be done in the same way as with the bridle.

The outside bend (away from the trainer) must come from the inside hand, since the effect of the outside rein on the nose, as opposed to the inside hand, is much less clear. Only as the training advances will the horse

The yellow arrow shows the application of the aids through the reins. The left, inside rein asks for the bend whilst the right, outside rein is lengthened so that the effect of the inside rein isn't restricted or blocked. The right hand can also be used on the neck to gently massage the neck while the handler should briskly stride forwards (red arrow).

The outside bend is initially created by the hand (here the left one) pressing the head away from the handler whilst shortening the right rein so than the contact isn't lost (yellow arrows). The handler's shoulders are turned towards the horse and he increases his pace slightly since he will be on the outside of the horse on the circle.

understand the aid through the outside rein more clearly, meaning that you can stop using the inside hand to press the neck away.

Stepping underneath on the circle

By now, thanks to the flexion exercises done both at halt and in walk, the forehand will have become supple and easy to direct, so that there is the necessary suppleness allowing for the gymnastic work to be continued through the quarters.

You now leave the larger circle and instead start to work on a volte or six- to ten-metre circle. The bend on a small circle must be clearer than before as the horse needs to step with his hind legs through towards his centre of gravity.

The horse's inside hip must be moved slightly further forward than the outside. Following correct preparatory work this should happen automatically. The trainer must not only control the bend, but must also control the quarters. The hand or the whip needs to be placed where the leg would normally be, in order to influence the movement of the hind legs, perfectly simulating a rider's leg.

The horse will place more weight on his inside hind leg, making it stronger and better able to carry the horse's weight, all of which help towards staying healthy. His centre of gravity moves slightly further back, putting less strain on his forehand, and he will feel better every day and able to enjoy his newly emerging self-confidence.

The most important role of this exercise consists of recognising the horse's centre of gravity and ensuring that the inside hind legs move towards it. Never forget that you are working on the edge of a horse's physical weight-bearing capability. For less supple horses, it is immensely difficult to take more strain through the hindquarters. Using in-hand work it is possible to demand more from the horse much faster, thanks to the lack of a rider's weight – but despite this, never overestimate the capability of your equine partner.

Only when you follow the principle, 'ask a little and praise a lot', will you be able to introduce these demands to a horse ensuring enjoyment and enthusiasm.

In order to encourage a horse to step through underneath his centre of gravity, enlarging the circle out of a ten-metre volte is an ideal exercise. Maintain a constant bend and step towards the horse's shoulder. To ensure that the hind leg steps under the centre of gravity you should place the whip or hand against the horse's side where the leg would normally lie. By asking the horse to move out on the circle the inner hip is automatically moved forward, and your hand is encouraging the inner hind leg to also move forwards and under the horse.

So that your hand can get the desired result, the aid must be given at exactly the right moment, which is just as the leg is lifted to step forwards. Only then is it off the ground and you, as trainer, have the chance to influence it. If the leg is on the ground then his weight will be on it and it will be impossible to have an effect.

When riding, the leg aids are more often than not given at the wrong moment and the rider then gets either annoyed or wonders why the horse doesn't respond enough or at all. From the horse's point of view, though, he is being asked to do something that he physically can't

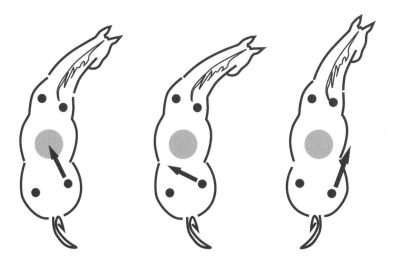

CENTRE OF GRAVITY

The large circles show where the centre of gravity lies, with the arrows showing the direction in which the inside hind leg is moving. The illustration at the far left shows that thanks to the placement of his hip, the horse's hind leg is stepping directly under his centre of gravity. At this moment, the horse has to take considerably more weight on this leg and is still developing its weight-bearing ability. The bend is correct, with the horse's spine curved; there is no S-bend, thanks to a slightly forward positioned hip, and as a result the horse is in perfect balance.

In the middle illustration you can see that the hind leg steps past behind the centre of gravity, resulting in the horse falling out through his quarters and avoiding taking the weight through his quarters – the result is that the horse steps short.

An incorrect hip alignment is shown in the third illustration: this does not allow the hind leg to step underneath the horse, stepping past and in front of it instead. This example is in fact what happens most frequently when a horse is trying to avoid stepping through. Young and stiff horses particularly tend towards this crooked movement, going against the bend at the same time.

do. To avoid this misunderstanding, the rider has to be able to feel his horse's movement and know at any moment what the hind leg is doing – not an easy thing to learn. When working a horse in-hand though, you are able to see what the horse is doing and see when the relevant hind leg is moving forward and can be influenced. As with leg aids, the whip shouldn't be used constantly, but rather be released when the leg is again on the ground.

Problem: the horse doesn't react

As discussed already, your timing must be perfect to ensure that the horse can respond

Stepping through and under

Here the horse is positioned and bent perfectly to prepare for him to step underneath his centre of gravity. The whip is used to activate the hind leg ...

... so that he places it well under himself and takes his weight. Ths ability of the horse to balance himself is improved enourmously with this exercise.

Thanks to the hip placement, the hindquarters come well through and the hind leg finds its optimal position – exactly where it belongs!

to your demands. If he doesn't respond to the aid from the whip asking him to step over, you can also use your hand. Most horses react much better to the hand than to the whip.

By using the inside of your hand laid flat against the horse, you also increase the number of options open to you: you can use a single finger and gently tickle the horse, or use the entire palm to create greater pressure. This option should over time,

and once the horse understands the command, be replaced with the whip.

To ensure that the horse doesn't get upset or excited, the whip should never be used as a punishment, but rather as an aid. If the horse doesn't respect the whip then you should return to using the hand.

Touching his hindquarters or leg with the whip is not appropriate at this stage, as it often results in the horse taking a shorter step. As an exception it may be used if the horse is

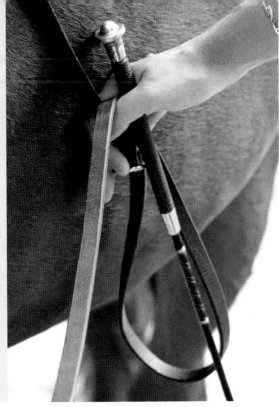

The whip and the back of the hand should touch the horse.

threatening to doze off or is too lazy and doesn't keep up with the trainer. With short and sharp touches with the whip you can 'liven up' the hind quarters, but using the whip to get the horse to step under himself can be counterproductive.

Problem: the horse steps through behind the centre of gravity.

As shown in the illustration, the position of the hip and the resulting direction that the inside hind leg takes are decisive in ensuring the correct bend in a volte. The horse must take a long step well under himself – stepping behind and past the centre of gravity will result in the horse taking a shorter step. In most cases the cause of this is an overreaction to the whip,

Alternatively you can also use the inside of your hand without the whip at all.

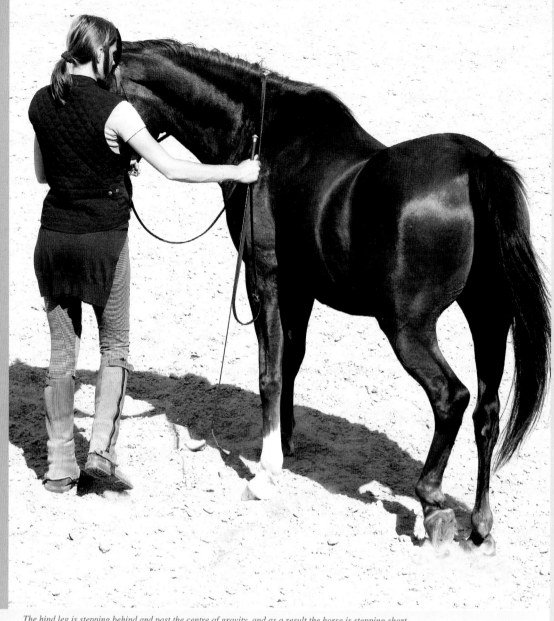

The hind leg is stepping behind and past the centre of gravity, and as a result the horse is stepping short.

when the horse pushes his whole croup to the outside and the hindquarters overtake the forehand. To counter this you must bring the forehand more to the outside and be more subtle with the whip aid.

At the moment when you approach the horse's shoulders, the whip should be passive so that the hindquarters aren't also pushed out. At the same time, you need to ensure

that the horse maintains an energetic tempo. Too much bend must be prevented through the outside rein.

Falling out through the quarters is a very bad fault and can be very difficult to correct, since there is obviously no rider's leg to be used. Only the edge of the manege and the control over the neck and shoulders are of help to the trainer. (See also 'What is the correct bend', on page 77).

Due to too little bend and a lack of impulsion,
the horse's left hind leg steps to the inside, past his centre of gravity.

Problem: the horse steps inside of and past his centre of gravity

Stepping on the inside of his centre of gravity is usually the result of too little bend. To correct this you need to better activate the hindlegs and use this to create a supple and even bend.

You need to bend and flex the horse, using the whip or the hand carefully when enlarging the circle so that the horse achieves the correct position though the hips and forehand.

How well a horse is able to step underneath himself also depends on his conformation. Short legs and poor hindquarters make stepping through more difficult. This is why it is very important to recognise any physical limitations that your horse may have.

Shoulder-in

The key exercise

The shoulder-in is the key exercise for suppling the horse. It loosens and frees the shoulders, trains the hindquarters to carry more weight, makes the horse's hips more mobile and refines the aids.

In the history of riding much has been said and written about the shoulder-in. Almost 400 years ago the Duke of Newcastle described a shoulder-in on a volte for the first time. The French riding master François Robichon de la Guérinière modified this lateral movement, using it on a straight line in order to loosen the horse's shoulders more. Gustav Steinbrecht has given a most exact treatment of the shoulder-in, which still applies today.

Today there is much dispute about the correct angle – whether a horse should go on three or four tracks – and depending on their point of view, people often form their own philosophy about this. This isn't an issue for in-hand work, as the goal aimed for and its correct execution will determine the angle.

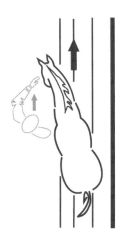

The shoulder-in on three...

...and four tracks.

The yellow line shows the actual bend in the form of an ellipse that comprises a series of straight lines but which doesn't run consistently along the spine.
The red line shows the consistent equivalent of the bend.
The blue line shows the ideal arc of a constant bend – although this is physically impossible.

It is impossible to maintain a deep bend at the withers through the entire horse. Here the elliptical curve is lost.

Regular bend?

One of the most fundamental requirements for shoulder-in is that the horse should show a regular bend through his entire hody. Although this sounds good in theory, in practice this is often elusivc, as it is impossible for a horse's spine to bend completely evenly. Especially through the thoracic (chest) vertebrae, sideways movement is minimal, and around the withers the spine is virtually impossible to bend, whilst in the neck it is the opposite, being very flexible. The bend that can be achieved resembles more an ellipse than an arc.

You can see from the principle of aiming for a regular bend, that the shoulder must be included in the movement, even if the bend through the neck is greater than that in the chest or loins. The horse must not be allowed to simply transfer his weight to the outside shoulder.

A deep bend through the neck is not counterproductive, but rather mirrors the initial work done at halt. The muscles on the outer side of the bend will be stretched and loosened, helping to develop the neck. Even if the bend stops before reaching the withers, it can still help the horse to loosen and relax. As long as there is something on the outside of the horse, such as a wall or edge of the school, then you

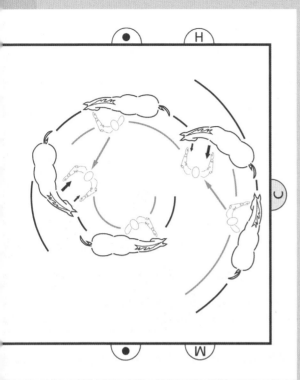

The moment at which you bring the horse towards you results in the desired lesson – the reins lead the shoulders to the inside. On the next and smaller circle you can bend and flex the horse anew and then again bring the shoulders in. By extending your arms you can ensure that the horse is left sufficient room.

time. The huge advantage offered by in-hand work is that you can also restrict the bend with the inside hand.

Preparation

By using the bending and flexing work, together with the work done to encourage the quarters to step under from behind in the volte, the horse is ideally prepared to go straight using the same balance. The majority of the preparation is already therefore done: on a circle the trainer is able to move the horse's shoulders to the outside and engage the quarter. Now it is time to move the shoulders to the inside, as the expression 'shoulder-in' clearly implies.

To do this you use an exercise which reduces the size of a circle. This exercise is specifically used as it enables you to better show the effect of the outside rein to the horse through moving the forehand. The focus of this exercise is on the horse's shoulders – for a moment you can ignore the hindquarters. The horse must learn that the trainer can bring the shoulders in by using inner bend and flexion. To do this start on a circle, bending and flexing the horse and begin to reduce the size of the circle. At the same time, bring the horse's shoulders more to the inside by using both reins. When doing this you can extend both arms out slightly, before pulling the shoulders towards you. The reduction in size in this exercise doesn't happen throughout the circle but rather at intervals: circle then bring the shoulders in; circle then bring the shoulders in.

should not have to worry about him falling out through his quarters. For lateral movements this bend would be much too great, though, as what you are trying to prevent would in fact occur – falling out through the shoulder.

Lateral movements do not demand great bending through the neck – this belongs to the work done when starting out. You can however go back to this if the horse becomes too tense and is no longer able to complete the lateral movements in a relaxed manner. In the lateral movements themselves the outer rein used to contain the bend through the neck, as when riding, will become more important over

Your distance from the horse together with slightly extended arms will initially keep the horse's shoulders to the outside...

...before bringing them in to the inside.

Execution

Now you are ready: The horse's shoulders can be moved to the inside and to the outside, the hindquarters can be engaged. The horse is now ready to carry out the shoulder-in on a straight line.

One way of developing this movement is by performing it out of a 20-metre circle onto a straight line. You only need to change the direction of movement whilst maintaining the bend from the circle.

On the circle the horse needs to be correctly flexed and bent. When you get to the outside track, you take one step into the school, moving the horse's shoulders over with you and proceed parallel to the track. The whip or your hand should rest on the girth line so that the inside hindleg steps straight under his centre of gravity – this should happen automatically when you change direction, as long as his shoulders are further in than his croup.

Praise your horse after the first few steps of shoulder-in, and then go back onto a circle to conclude the exercise.

The circle is also a useful tool if the horse goes too high in the poll through shoulder-in and tenses his neck muscles. A horse like this will need to be loosened up and encouraged to take the rein down before starting again.

You can also start the shoulder-in from the corner or a small circle. The degree of bend from the exercise before determines the quality of the shoulder-in. Since on a ten-metre circle the horse is bent much more, as long as he doesn't change the bend, he will automatically go into a shoulder-in with four tracks: 'Out of the previous lesson comes the next.' This principle runs through the entire training life of a horse and allows you to recognise in advance what the quality of the following exercises will be. This is why it is so important to carefully prepare for the shoulder-in.

The shoulder-in can be developed out of the circle.

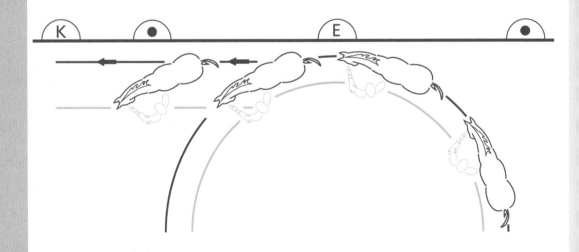

The horse's inside hind steps towards the outside fore – he is therefore working on three tracks. The bend stays consistent with the horse looking towards the middle of the school and the shoulders at a 30 degree angle to the perimeter of the school.

With horses who tend to run out through the shoulder, this particular lateral movement may prove to be a real challenge. They must not be allowed to bend too much, as this allows the whole shoulder to move onto the inside track.

The contact on the outside rein must be supported by the contact on the inside rein.

If the forehand starts to point towards the middle of the school, then the control through the reins must be clear and precise. Otherwise you will find that the horse is bent only through the neck, and the rest of his body stays on one track with additional weight on the shoulder which makes a mockery of the exercise.

Especially with larger warmblood horses the bend may make it seem as if a shoulder-in is being performed, and this is especially difficult to recognise from the saddle. Too often, the horse's neck is simply placed to the inside, with no actual control over the shoulders.

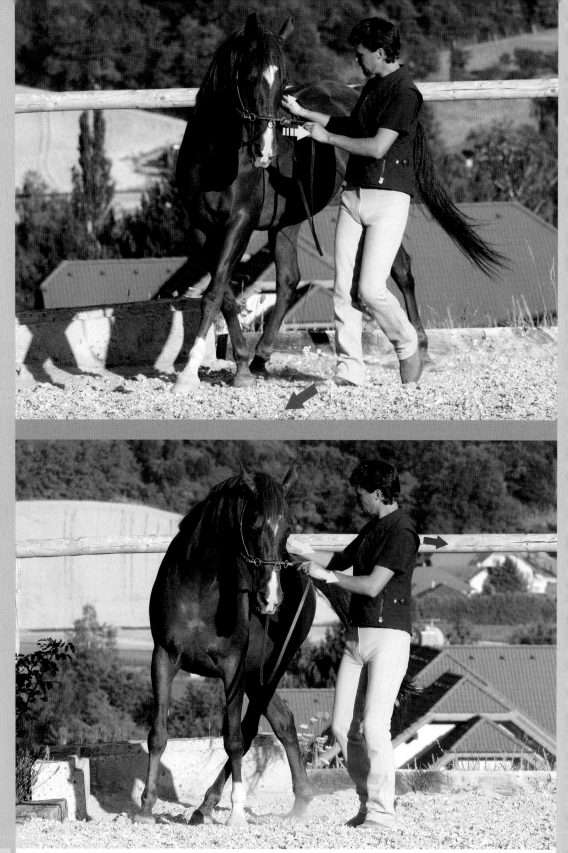

USING A LUNGEING CAVESSON

The shoulder-in can be carried out just as well with a lungeing cavesson, as long as the horse has done all of the preparatory work also without a bit. The inside rein is used to bend and flex the horse and the outside rein must be lengthened until the required level of bend is achieved (yellow arrow). The half-halts must result in the horse being in self-carriage, without which a correct shoulder-in is unthinkable. Should the horse not be so easy to bend and flex, go onto a ten-metre circle to relieve any resistance.

The direction taken by the trainer determines that of the horse (red arrow).

The blue arrow in the second picture shows that the trainer is having to lean back slightly in order to allow the horse sufficient room. The horse's forehand doesn't leave the track and there is a danger that he is going to stick to the outside of the school.

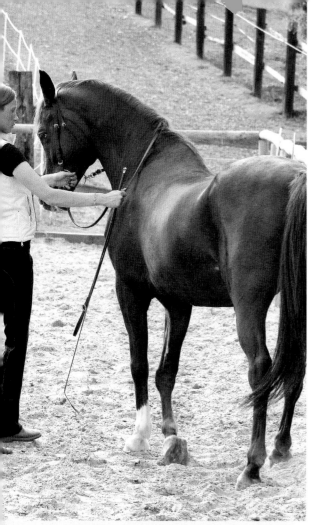

In the shoulder-in on four tracks the horse must not be put under pressure. The distance between the trainer and horse must be big enough to allow the hand holding the whip enough room to apply the aids precisely. The horse should move freely and in self-carriage throughout this difficult exercise.

stretched down the outside; although his hind legs no longer step under his centre of gravity, due to the shorter strides they do come underneath the body. In trot the horse starts to prepare for collection, and with in-hand work the shoulder-in on four tracks is very important, as it develops a trot which from the ground is very easy to work with. Broadly, you can say that thanks to the bend required, the shoulder-in at the walk loosens the horse, whilst in trot it collects.

Counter-shoulder-in

When executing a shoulder-in on four tracks, it can happen that the horse tries to move towards the centre of the manege, coming out of position and potentially cutting you off. The simplest way to stop this is the counter-shoulder-in: the outside track restricts the direction, the hand holding the whip determines the angle, increasing it if necessary.

The horse is bent around the handler and looks to the outside of the manege. The forehand should be on the inside track, the croup on the next track in, with the outside track reserved for the handler.

This version of shoulder-in may be done at a greater angle, i.e. on four tracks. It is different to the conventional shoulder-in only at the corners, otherwise it is in principle exactly the same and the effect of the counter-shoulder-in is only different on the circle or through corners. It is important to ensure that the angle isn't too great, otherwise the horse may not be able to cross his legs over in front, and may stumble. The handler will need to

Shoulder-in on four tracks
In the case of a shoulder-in on four tracks, if you stand behind the horse you will see that each leg leaves its own print and the shoulders are well into the school (the angle of his body to the long side will be about 45 degrees).

This version of the shoulder-in is often dismissed, yet it does have considerable advantages. The horse's body is extremely walk slightly faster because he has further to go than the horse. It is best to start this exercise by changing the rein out of the corner at the end of the long side. As the forehand almost reaches the outside track, push the hindquarters sideways under his body so they do not reach the track. So that you don't lose the bend, keep him angled to the outside of the school. It is important that you don't allow the horse to squeeze the trainer to the outside: a certain distance must be respected. Using this exercise, the horse will grasp the shoulder-in on four tracks very quickly and will soon be able to carry it out down the centre line.

Exercises for further development

For in-hand work, the shoulder-in and its counter exercise are very important. Especially the work on four tracks will prove to be difficult since when working in an indoor school some horses find the close presence of the wall threatening. It is therefore to be recommended that at the start the angle to the track is 30 degrees, using a steeper angle when working within the school. One particular exercise combines these elements and helps to establish any angle required.

The exercise comprises a shoulder-in on three tracks, then moving into an approximately six-metre circle, shoulder-in on four tracks on a straight line away from the track, followed by a ten-metre circle. For the trainer it demands precision and co-ordination in the application of the aids, and simultaneous control of the shoulders and quarters.

When practising the counter-shoulder-in, the horse must not press to the outside track.

1. *Shoulder-in on the long side:*
   Beginning in the corner place the horse into shoulder-in on three tracks and continue for a few metres.

2. *Move onto a volte:* Now comes a significant moment – the trainer must try to bring the hindquarters around on a half circle to the outside. This is the same as the exercise to step through on a circle (see page 83) – with the difference that you don't move the shoulders to the outside, but rather bring them towards you. The forehand is kept to the inside, and the quarters turn the greatest distance. The inside hind steps slightly behind the centre of gravity so that the hindquarters are closer to the centre line that the forehand.

   The inside flexion should remain the same as in the shoulder-in, while the combination of the aids through the reins and whip should ideally be the reins bringing the shoulder further to the inside, but at the same time the hand holding the whip pushing the croup round in a wide circle. The hindquarters are thus swung round until the angle is reached which creates the shoulder-in on four tracks.

3. *Shoulder-in parallel to the long side:* After the bend, the trainer changes direction and follows a line parallel to the long side. The shoulder-in now proceeds on four tracks. The tempo should have been set on the half-circle and must not increase as you move along the school. Half-halts on the outside rein, a calm voice and a steady pace will quickly bring the horse back to the required speed. This mirrors the counter-shoulder-in done along the outside track, with the difference that the track is somewhat further away, although it still acts to slow the movement down. It is important that you remain straight and steady so as not to make the horse insecure.

4. *Half-circle:* The conclusion of this exercise is a half-circle to return back to the outside track, where the exercise can be started again.

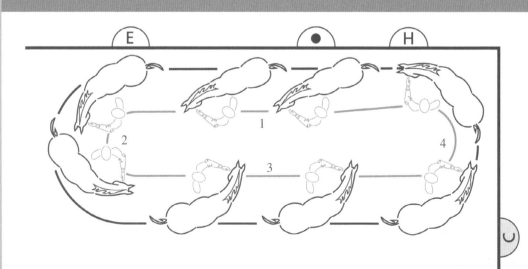

You should not expect to get this perfect at the first attempt. But after a few tries your horse should have grasped what you want and it should become easier – the same applies to the trainer, who will need to learn to apply the aids with increased finesse. Another variation of this exercise is the square circle, with every straight side being joined by a quarter circle. The angle in the shoulder-in can be varied on every side, being set up through the corners.

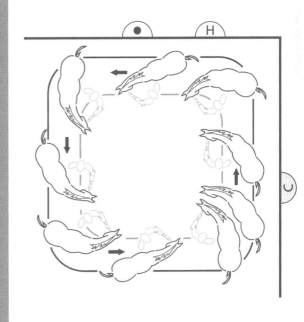

In trot

A horse's walk is normally slightly faster than your own walk. With turns and circles, this difference can usually be overcome and some of the forward energy can be used by the horse to carry himself. The trot however is a pace that can't be maintained by a person on the ground for any length of time.

A solution for this challenge can be found by utilising lateral movements which require the horse to take shorter strides: the shorter the length of stride, the slower the speed, without causing the horse to drag his feet or go on the forehand. To start to bring the trot into the work done in-hand, the counter-shoulder-in makes an ideal exercise. The outer edge of the school stops the horse from going too quickly; the whip controls the angle of the hindquarters and can ensure the horse moves forwards – not just sideways but also forwards.

By carrying this out on four tracks the horse will step through from behind shorter, whilst the bend will keep him supple and the outside of the school will control his speed – meaning that even on the most forward-going of horses, you should be able to avoid using too much force to slow him down.

Horses do adapt quickly to the desired speed, so you shouldn't be towed around. The horse shouldn't run into trot, but instead should take longer strides. Running into a pace only encourages a horse to go faster, and can in some cases result in a horse seeing it as a game, and going yet faster.

SUMMARY

When starting it is very important that the horse trots for only a short period, and when he obeys the command, finish the exercise and praise him.

The horse must recognise that he has done what has been asked of him correctly, an impression that is strengthened by praise, and this will encourage him to reproduce the trot again and again as required.

Transitions into and out of trot

For the trot carried out in counter-shoulder-in, you must build up a degree of tension in your own body that will help the horse through the transition. Following this, you should take a longer stride and give the voice command to trot on. If not before, then at least following a light touch of the whip – either on the girth or, exceptionally, on the quarters – the horse should trot on.

The correct sequence of the aids can be described as follows:

1. Tense your own body
2. Move forward
3. Voice
4. Whip.

Again the principle followed should be to use 'as much as necessary and as little as possible'.

Especially in the trot, it is important that the horse doesn't crowd his handler on the outside track. Respect for people should already be well-established in his training. In order that the horse doesn't try to move his hindquarters

Also in the trot the inner rein asks for the bend and the outside rein is in a light contact and determines the required lengthening. With this horse, who is already secure in trot, the whip is held passively since he needs no additional encouragement to trot on.

from the required track, the inside rein should create slightly more bend and the whip should at the same time ask for a greater angle on the movement. The aids to transition back to walk are comparable to those for halting. Mostly, all you will need to do is to breathe in deeply, supported by a long drawn-out command, 'Waaaalk!'.

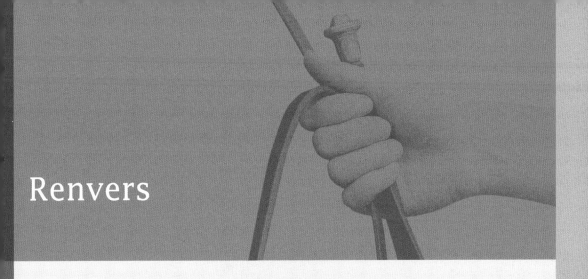

Renvers

Preparation

For in-hand work the renvers is practised before the related exercise, the travers. The trainer should be on the third track, with the horse's forehand on the second and his hindquarters on the outside (first) track. The horse should be facing the direction of the movement and be bent in the same direction.

The renvers as seen from behind
The handler is located on the outside of her horse, with the left hand controlling the outside rein, the right the inside as well as the whip. The horse is looking in the same direction as the movement and is bent to the right.

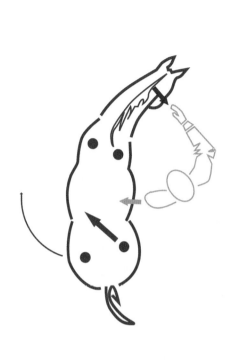

Bend and flexion to the inside (red arrow) as well as the aids with the whip-holding hand (grey arrow) cause the horse's hind quarter to move round.

The exercises described in this book originate from the French school of riding. Through the incorporation of bending and flexion, in-hand work will immediately increase the need for balance before starting to move off, and not the opposite.This is an important point as our four-legged friends have a great advanatage over us when it comes to forwards movement. Suppling and training must therefore be achieved using other methods – through stretching and loosening of the muscles, specially designed movements and development of the weight-bearing ability. The French

school of riding serves to build on these basic principles primarily from the saddle, but when working from the ground elements of these are highlighted, allowing a horse to benefit greatly. François Baucher, the French riding master, developed a very good exercise which opens the way for a horse to learn the renvers – considered to be a very difficult lateral movement.

In only a few steps it prepares the horse to (unlike the shoulder-in) bring his outside hind leg underneath his body and to move in the direction of his bend.

Step 1:
Turn on the forehand

One thing should be clear from the start. This exercise is the means to an end, and not an end in itself. Normally one should never ask a horse's inside hind leg to step through and past its centre of gravity, but this is an exception. At a halt the horse should be bent and flexed to the inside so that the whip-holding hand can then be placed slightly behind the girth to gently push it around.

The hindlegs should step around the forehand, barely moving from the spot. If the horse doesn't understand the aids to move sideways, it is possible to increase the bend whilst at the same time using your hand or fingers to push on his stomach to help him to understand what is required. This selective aid mostly does the job and should already be known by the horse from being groomed, as when being groomed he needs to be able to move his quarters over to the left or the right.

As soon as the horse responds to the pressure from either the whip or fingers, the aid should be immediately stopped and only be used when next required.

The inside rein holds the horse's head to the inside and must be prepared to give when the horse reacts as asked. The outside rein must stay in contact even when the aids for the sideways movements are given.

Step 2:
Expansion

Once the horse allows his quarters to be moved over then you are a step closer to performing the renvers. At halt, ensure that the horse is straight, and get him to move his quarters over.

What is different here is that you should begin to change around the aids given. As an expansion on the turn on the forehand, the inside rein becomes the outside, and vice versa. The aid driving the horse forwards, though, stays the same. The whip or your hand should push the quarters around the forehand. The role of the inside rein is to stop the horse bending to the inside – since he will be used to doing this for the turn on the forehand, he is likely to try immediately to do this. The inside rein and outside hands are therefore responsible for keeping the horse's head as straight as possible, while also encouraging the hindquarters to yield.

Managing both the rein and the whip in one hand will be a challenge initially for the inexperienced handler. The hand must be used lower down so that the rein has the correct effect whilst also being used to create forwards movement – a real test for anyone trying in-hand work. The most important support is that of the other hand, which needs to keep the horse's head straight.

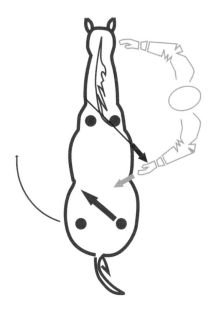

The hand holding the rein and the whip together has a double role to play: with the rein to prevent any bend (red arrow), and at the girth to encourage the hindquarters to move around (grey arrow).

Step 3:
Renvers on a small circle

The horse should now be flexed towards the direction he is moving on a small circle (10 m). The hindquarters should therefore be describing a larger circle than his forehand. This is the completion of a turn on the forehand done with forwards movement. The aids have changed around so that the horse is bent away from the trainer, and what was previously the inside hindleg has become the outside hind – a renvers is born!

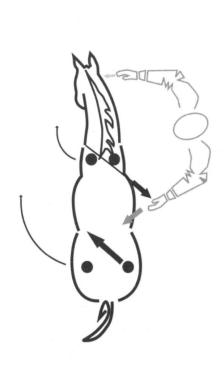

The natural result of good preparation: a renvers with the correct bend and flexion.

The change of the inside to the outside rein is now complete. The handler controls the degree of flexion and bend with the new inside rein, whilst the outside rein continues to act in a supporting role.

You, as the handler, should complete a small circle, setting the horse in motion to also complete a circle. Gradually the circle can be made larger, always ensuring that the hindquarters are travelling the greatest distance.

Renvers in a straight line

Just as the shoulder-in is a key exercise for suppling and gymnasticising your horse, so is the renvers another building block for a healthy, self-confident and motivated horse. The renvers can influence a horse's expression and bearing so much that you would think you were looking at a different horse. The ability to carry himself through his quarters will be increased, and the bending and stretching of his muscles that this exercise demands will help to create a much more impressive-looking horse, with a more elevated forehand.

The renvers also completes the aids for the in-hand work. Once he has practised this particular lateral movement, he will be familiar with many of the different commands, he will better understand their purpose and will be ready, also under saddle, to carry out the different movements. In other words, once your in-hand work has reached the stage of renvers, the way is open for all other movements. You just have to take the first step …

The easiest way to build up to renvers on a straight line is to simply continue on the renvers

The aids to create the impulsion are exactly the same as before. The whip however now encourages the outside hind underneath the horse's body. In doing this the timing is important: at the moment when the hindleg is about to leave the ground, the whip or hand needs to be applied to encourage the leg forwards and sideways under his body. As soon as the horse responds, relax the aid and only apply again for the next step. There should be a clear sequence of applying the aid, releasing and then re-applying for each step.

In renvers a horse's experssion and outline can benefit greatly.

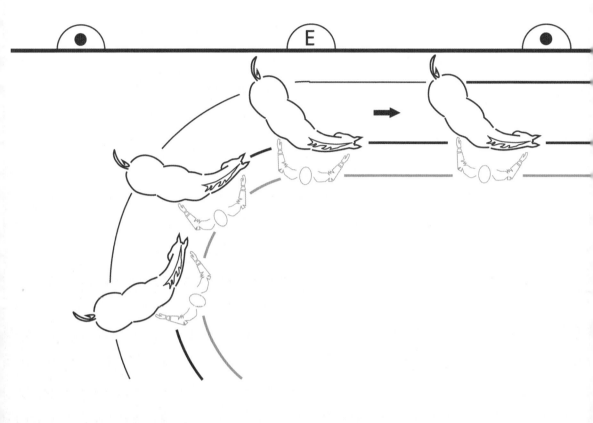

It should be relatively easy to turn the renvers on the circle into renvers on a straight line.

on a circle up the outside track. What is vital here is for the trainer to hold his own line down the track once he comes out of the curve in the corner. The outside of the manege will help keep the direction so that this particular exercise should not be hard for either horse or handler.

When working in-hand the renvers should be carried out on four tracks, although in walk this will be very collected. Due to the shorter, collected steps and the elevated forehand created by the renvers, the way is also open to collected trot. Before trying this in trot however, the renvers in walk needs to be secure and the horse needs to be relaxed and accepting of both the rein and whip aids. The horse must also have plenty of room to truly show that he can attain the angle that is being asked of him.

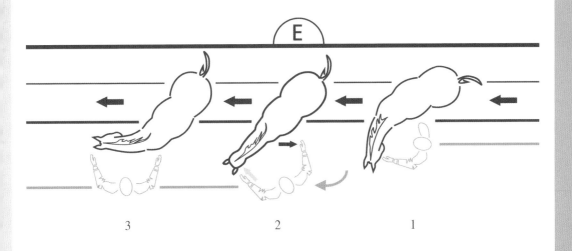

SHOULDER-IN TO RENVERS

Another option coming from renvers is changing the bend out of shoulder-in. To do this proceed down the long side on the outside track in shoulder-in at a steep angle in an almost slow-motion walk. Now begin to change the bend. Very carefully take up the outside rein using gentle half-halts to change the bend towards the direction of movement (red arrow). The inside rein (yellow arrow) supports but allows this. The whip is placed slightly behind the girth and continues to drive the inside hindleg sideways.

At the same time the handler should take a big step inwards from the outside track (grey arrow) so that, despite the stretching of the neck muscles away from her, the contact with the horse's mouth is not lost.

By the end, the aids have changed around, the horse is rebalanced, bending away from the handler and is moving in renvers down the long side.

This way of using the renvers is not only very elegant, but it allows gifted horses a way of developing their skills rapidly. Despite this, you must be careful with this method to ensure that the horse properly changes the bend through his entire body and doesn't just bend through his neck. Especially with a horse with a short neck, it will be difficult to develop the renvers in this way. They can set themselves in such a way that it is impossible to change the aids around to make the outside, the inside rein. The best way to do this is using the renvers out of the volte.

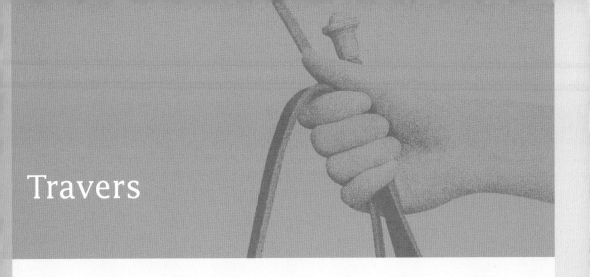

Travers

Preparation

The travers differs from the renvers only in so far as the horse's head, rather than his quarters, is on the outside track. In travers the horse is also flexed and bent in the direction of the movement but his hindquarters are on the inside. The handler is located on the outside track, the horse's forehand on the second and the hindquarters on a third track.

The shallow angle of the travers makes a more gentle bend through the body possible. The outside hind reaches well under the centre of gravity and takes a considerable amount of weight through it. In contrast to the case of renvers on four tracks, or the half-pass, the forelegs cross over as well and the horse is bent more through the neck than in the rest of his body. The danger then arises that the horse

Travers is carried out on three tracks. The hindlegs cross over and the forehand should be positioned slightly in front.

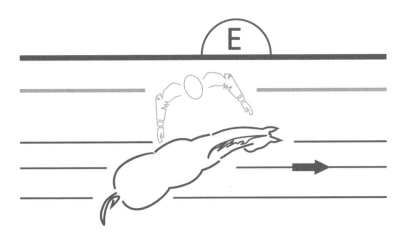

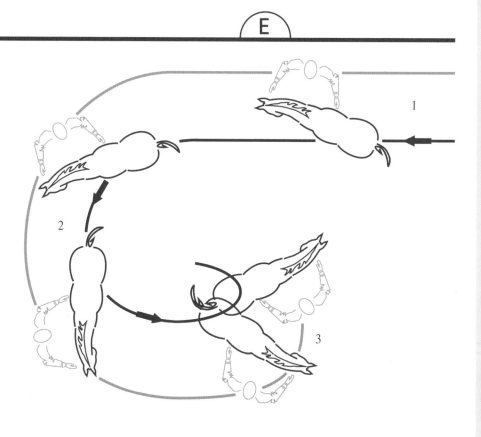

Travers in a straight line (1), followed by a volte (2), turning into a walk pirouette (3).

is only bent through the neck and the inside hip isn't truly engaged and moved through and forward. It is different though in the case of a horse with a shorter back: in this case the angle can be greater since due to the shorter back, it will be less likely to pass through its centre of gravity.

Since the outside track is reserved for the handler, being located on the horse's outside, the inside leg is in effect missing in this lateral movement. For this reason you must be careful that the croup doesn't move over too much into the middle of the manege. Should this occur, move forwards again quickly and reduce the bend.

A horse that is secure in renvers should not have any problems with travers, and can soon be working towards walk pirouette.

From travers on the circle to walk pirouette

The pirouette also has a purpose. It should be used to collect, lift the forehand and strengthen the hindquarters. As with all the other exercises it is used as a means to an end – the end being a more balanced horse. From the horse's perspective, all that is happening throughout these varying exercises is that his balance is being moved and changed. You are helping the horse into a position that allows him to carry out various movements using different areas of balance – also the case in the walk pirouette.

Working towards this from the travers on a straight line, move onto a volte in the corner of the manege. The horse must stay on the circle, with his hind legs making the smaller of circles. The volte is reduced in size until you end up by completing a pirouette in walk.

Using this exercise you can control the outside hind leg, which needs to step well under the body and fully show off its gymnastic potential.

Providing that this exercise is prepared for properly, it should be easy to carry out. In this case the reduction in the size of the circle needs to be carefully worked through as this then becomes the pirouette, or in other words a turn on the hindquarters.

The tempo of the travers on the circle must be very slow, controlling every individual step. and be in a position to be able to halt the horse at any moment. Unlike the travers in a straight line, the angle must be greater but the bend through the neck must not increase, since the pirouette leads to a greater lifting of the forehand which may be blocked if the bend in the neck is too great. The more the horse lifts in front, the less bent the neck should be.

The whip actively controls the outside hind leg – but its application should be slightly earlier than normal. This exercise works clearly towards collection, and the horse must be encouraged to actively step with his hind legs. The whip should be used just before his outside hind leg leaves the ground, encouraging it to do so quickly.

The smaller the circle becomes, the more the handler will need to turn himself in towards the horse's neck. The horse's forehand should make a larger circle around the hindquarters and the handler must, because he is located on the outside of the horse's forehand, go with the horse on the circle. The usual position at the shoulder will need to be given up, moving instead closer to the horse's head. In the walk pirouette the handler should always walk forwards and sideways.

When doing this for the first time it is important to lift the horse up in front. As in the basic work, this can be achieved by taking up a firmer contact on the reins upwards towards the corner of the horse's mouth which also acts to hold him.

Actively lifting up the horse's neck and outline in this way in conventional riding is one of the taboos, because there is concern that the horse may hollow his back. In the French school of riding however, this is almost overdone and constitutes a corner-stone of the tradition.

For in-hand work a middle path should be taken. The horse should understand the aid to lift the forehand. When required, as is the case here, the trainer can use this aid in order to assist his horse with the exercise.

Once you are on the decreasing circle you should give an upwards half-halt. The horse should respond by lifting his neck upwards from his withers. The forwards aids need to be kept active so that the horse understands that he not only needs to lift the forehand but also keep active through through his quarters.

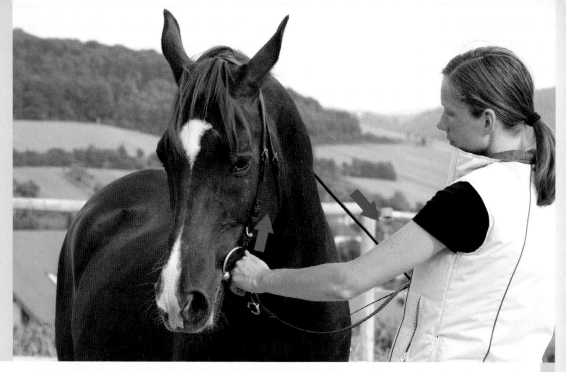

These aids are necessary for the pirouette

The red arrow shows the upwards half-halt on the outside rein. It lifts the horse's forehand whilst also holding and containing him. The blue arrow indicates the contact with the inside rein. Taking up a stronger contact creates the bend which is supported by the other hand.

The whip (yellow arrow) may, as an exception, be used on the horse's flanks. The trainer needs to stand up straight and then consistently and deliberately take the forehand around the horse's hindquarters.

You shouldn't demand too much, however, when beginning to work on the pirouette. Only ask for two or three steps and then stop immediately so the horse can stretch down. Clear praise for a job well done will help to cement the lesson.

If the horse starts to turn around the hind leg instead of stepping – lifting it and putting it back down – enlarge the circle straight away, go back to the travers and start over again. How much the circle should be reduced by depends on the horse. Don't go too far too soon; reduce it by only a few metres – in this case less is often more!

Only when the horse is experienced in reducing the size of the circle should you go that step further. As initially indicated, it isn't imperative that you achieve the perfect pirouette. Getting there provides all of the suppling exercises that a horse needs.

Travers out of shoulder-in

Another option to develop this movement is to develop travers out of the shoulder-in on the outside track. The advantage of this is that you don't need to change the bend. The bend in travers is the same as in shoulder-in. The entire body is shifted around so that the shoulders in the same bend is brought onto the outside track. In doing this the trainer moves his outside hand up towards the horse's neck, turns his outside shoulder in towards the horse, in effect turning on his own axis. Since the horse maintains the same bend he rebalances immediately into the travers,

Out of the shoulder in (1) the horse moves step by step into the travers.

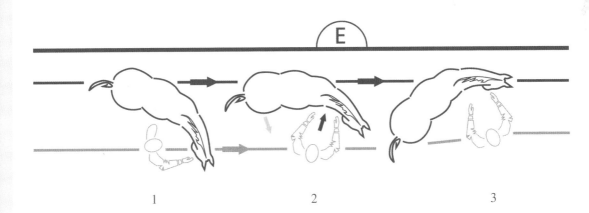

1   2   3

During shoulder-in the angle must not be too great, to ensure that you do not have to bring the shoulders too far off the track and so that the horse's inside hip really is further forward that the outer.

whereby his hindquarters will automatically move into the manege on the new track. The trainer is still on the inside of the horse, is holding the horse's shoulders on the track and is better able to control the bend and the flexion.

The disadvantage is that you do need something to the outside to act as a barrier. This type of travers is really only suitable for the outside track and is usually only used to help to straighten the horse in piaffe. In all other cases the position on the horse's offside tends to be preferred.

In order to shift his body over, you need to turn your upper body away from the direction of the movement at the same time pointing towards the horse's shoulder. You create the gentle bend by resting a hand against the neck.

The change from shoulder-in to travers has worked. You should now be walking backwards, maintaining the bend with your left hand on his neck. The arm is stretched out to keep the horse at the correct distance with the outside of the manege, creating a natural barrier to the outside.

Half-pass

The inner picture

The half-pass is very closely related to the travers and renvers. The horse will already understand both of these movements and should therefore be able to quickly learn the half-pass.

The real difficulty lies in problems of containment. The movement of the half-pass takes place in the middle of the manege, with no outer boundary to help the horse, only the handler being to the outside.

In the half-pass the horse is bent and flexed towards the direction of the movement. The angle is the same as in the renvers – four tracks, with the front and back legs crossing over. As with the ridden half-pass, the forehand should lead – in other words, when looking at it from the front or above, the forehand should be slightly in front on the hindquarters in the direction of the movement.

The half-pass to the left. From the chest back, the body should be almost parallel to the long side.

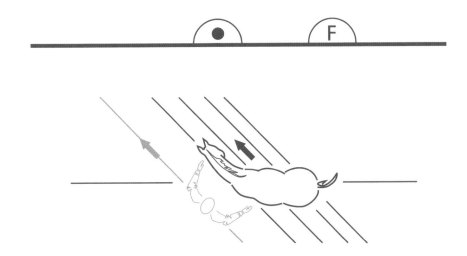

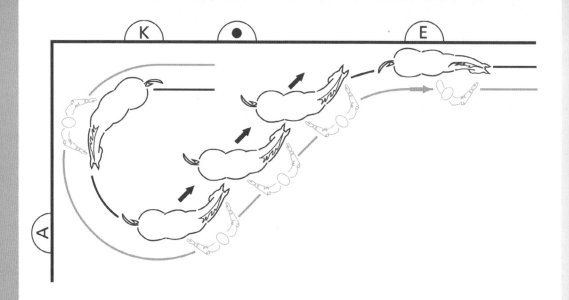

Pass out of a change of rein out of the corner.

This lateral movement is carried out on a diagonal parallel to the long side. It is hugely important to understand in your own head what is required – it simplifies the exercise greatly. The inner picture' of a half-pass will ensure that the lesson is carried out correctly. Also it enables you to be able to focus on the edge of the manege and aim for this point. Once the horse is clear about where he is required to go, the preparation provided by the other lateral movements will help him to be able to perform the half-pass successfully.

Preparation and execution

The simplest way of developing the half-pass is to perform it through a change of hand. Changing the rein out of the corner is best suited for this because the distance back to the outside track is relatively short, and so the horse doesn't have far to go in half-pass when starting out.

The handler must place himself to the outside on the long side, so that he is correctly positioned for the half-pass. He will then be positioned on the inside of the horse to go back up the long side. To prepare, a half ten-metre circle should be started. The horse should be bent away from the handler so that he reaches a line parallel to the long side in this position, with the hindquarters then being pushed sideways. This will cause the outside hindleg to step sideways and forwards well under his body. The reins control the shoulder, the whip the croup. The horse should then half-pass on a diagonal line to the outside track, and once meeting the track should be bent to the inside.

Once the horse has mastered the sideways movement you should concentrate on the horse going forwards so that the half-pass is carried out with even more impulsion. By doing this the horse will gradually learn to maintain the impulsion and the forwards tendency.

Any necessary corrections at this stage of the training will happen automatically. The horse's

The half-pass – an advanced test for any horse.

shoulders may need to be moved to the right or left, or the quarters may need to be encouraged through more to correct the angle. Your own eye will by this time be trained to recognise what is correct, so it is just a matter of more practice to gain more expresson from the horse in order to encourage him to even higher levels of self-confidence.

Through these lessons the horse should now be in perfect balance and soon ready to start the more advanced 'High School' movements – if required. Whatever you decide to do, the newly won balance and suppleness will benefit your horse not just in the manege but also in his quality of life.

HALF-PASS IN TROT

Once the counter-shoulder-in has been accomplished in trot and the horse has become used to completing the movement at this pace, there is nothing to stand in the way of carrying out all the lateral movements in trot. With every practice, the horse will be closer to achieving collected trot. Completing a good half-pass in trot is a real achievement in the training of any horse – a sentiment felt by the horse as well as by his trainer.

Half-pass using the lungeing cavesson

The greatest difficulty in carrying out the half-pass using a lungeing cavesson is achieving and maintaining the correct bend away from the handler. To do this a horse that

Although the horse is crossing his hind and fore legs, he is too straight. With a relaxed wrist, the left hand (yellow arrow) needs to lead towards the ground in a pulsing movement to bend the horse more. At the same time it controls the shoulder so that the angle, in connection with the whip isn't lost. The right hand (red arrow) supports the left.

responds lightly to the change of bend is indispensable. The cavesson can only give signals to help the horse into the new bend. As long as you still need to use the whip-holding hand to create bend, it is too early to attempt the half-pass. Go back to circles and voltes positioned to the outside of the horse so that it becomes second nature for him to bend and flex away from his handler. Only then can you move onto the half-pass.

After correction a good half-pass is shown with correct bend.

Combining lateral movements

A multitude of variations

The combination of lateral movements is the very essence of gymnastic exercises. Now that the horse has mastered all the lateral movements, you can work on perfecting them. The variations are endless. Only the position of the handler to the left or right of the horse limits the possibilities. You cannot be on the outside of the horse in shoulder-in and on the inside in travers. For this reason you should be confident about which combinations are open to you to use, and from which side of the horse.

In the following section a number of examples will be shown connecting the various movements which may be carried out in-hand as well as when ridden. They are recommended for experienced and advanced horses, and pose a great challenge for both horse and handler. Parts of them can however also be used for less experienced partnerships. If this is the case, then when starting, sections of the movement should be practised in isolation, step-by-step, before combining them in their entirety.

It is also important to correctly judge a horse's capabilities, so as not to demand too much too soon. It is often better to work on a ten-metre circle instead of a pirouette, rather than cause too much strain on a horse's muscles. Nonetheless, the following exercises will be both mentally and physically demanding for both horse and handler. The fast transitions from one lateral movement into the next are an enormous effort for the brain.

Gymnastic exercises develop not just the body but also the mind!

Triple-loop serpentines incorporating lateral movements.

Begin with shoulder-in on the short side using the same bend on the first loop. After the first loop in the middle of the school the horse should be straightened, before moving into travers on the second loop. The hindquarters must describe the shorter distance, with the horse bent away from the trainer, who is on the outside of the horse. The horse is straightened again after this and before entering the third loop the horse needs to be flexed to the inside so that he is in the correct position and angle for the final loop. Almost at the end of the

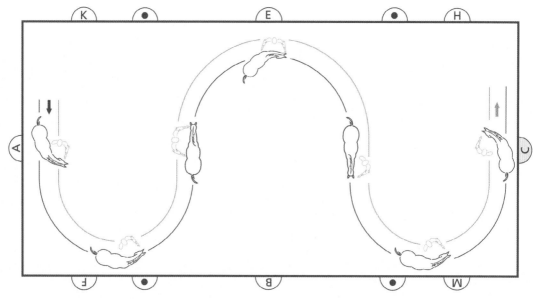

Triple-loop serpentine with lateral movements

final loop the shoulders are brought slightly more to the inside, so that the forehand almost starts a ten-metre circle, then move back to shoulder-in on the short side once again.

Single- and double-loop serpentines

With the single-loop serpentine particular attention should be paid to the half-pass movement in the second half. Just as you reach the point where the bend must change (1), introduce the half-pass (2). You just need to ask the hindquarters over and you have the half-pass. The double-loop serpentine offers two possibilities to incorporate lateral movements: after the corner, do not change the bend but as you change the direction a shoulder-in results almost automatically (3) on a short diagonal to the wall. From there (4) start the second loop into the school and at its apex change the bend and ask a few steps of half-pass (5).

Figures of eight with lateral movements

The circle is well-suited for practising a combination of lateral movements on curves: ask for the first circle in shoulder-in and the second in travers. This is the simplest way to connect these two movements. The line across the middle of the eight is particularly important as here the horse should always be straightened and prepared for the next movement.

Two further combinations on the figure of eight are:

- shoulder-in on the first circle, counter-shoulder-in on the second
- travers on the first circle, renvers on the second.

Neither of these variations need the horse to be straightened in the middle, as the bend and flexion don't change, just the direction.

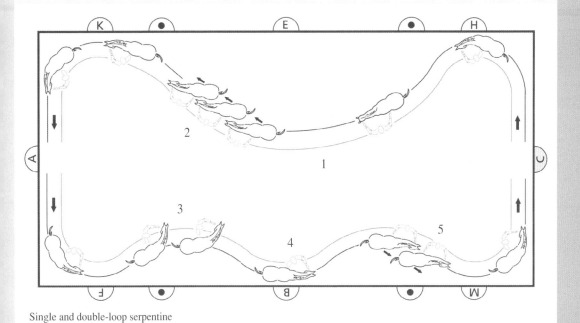

Single and double-loop serpentine

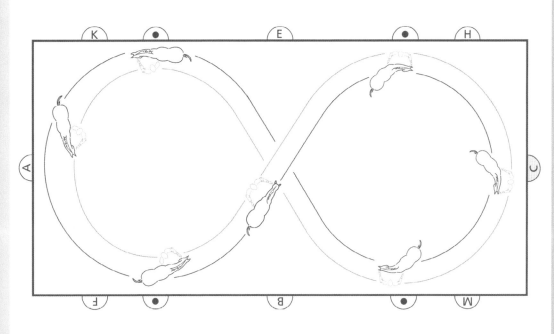

Figure of eight

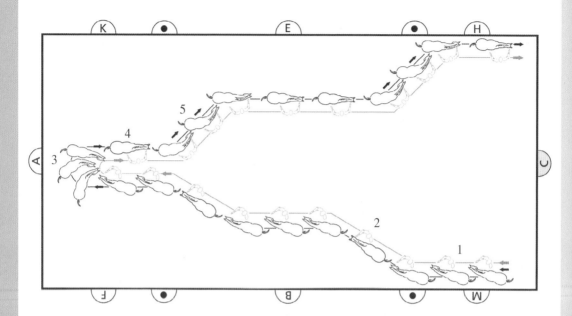

Shoulder-in and half-pass

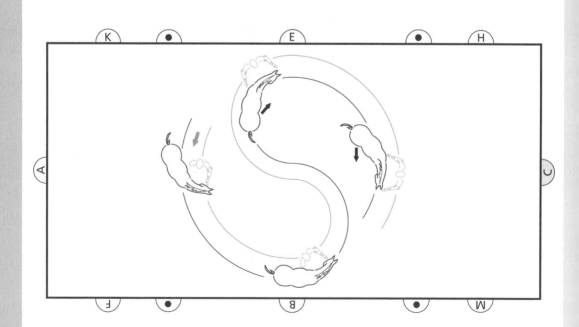

Changing the rein through the circle incorporating lateral movements

Shoulder-in and half-pass

From the shoulder-in (1) walk towards the centre of the school, making certain he is straight on the short diagonal (2). Then follows another few steps in shoulder-in. At the end of the school do a turn on the forehand (3), and then after a few steps straight ahead (4) move to half-pass (5). Repeat this to meet the outside track.

Changing the rein through the circle incorporating lateral movements

Changing the rein through the circle provides the opportunity to combine two different movements. Start shoulder-in on the circle and at the point of changing the rein through the middle of the circle alter the bend, and before the hindquarters start the new circle, allow the croup to go sideways, creating travers on the circle. Further variations of this exercise are changing from renvers to travers or from counter-shoulder-in to shoulder-in. In these cases the bend isn't changed through the centre of the circle, which makes it much easier.

Triangles

Containing two diagonal lines and a straight one, a triangle provides a great opportunity to combine lateral movements and turns.

Start with a shoulder-in on three tracks (1) and increase the angle to create a shoulder-in on four tracks (2), then change the bend for renvers (3). The direction the horse is travelling in doesn't change, only the bend and flexion. The aids change and you now find yourself on the horse's outside. A renvers turn follows (4) and when the correct angle is reached, then half-pass can be started across the diagonal (5). At the end of the diagonal the horse should be straightened and on the corner of the triangle do a quarter ten-metre circle (6). On the final diagonal the horse should walk in straight line (7), and just before reaching the track move into shoulder-in, and complete another quarter circle (8) to complete the triangle and finish on the outside track.

This exercise can be carried out in a number of variations, with the handler's position to the inside or outside creating the lines of the

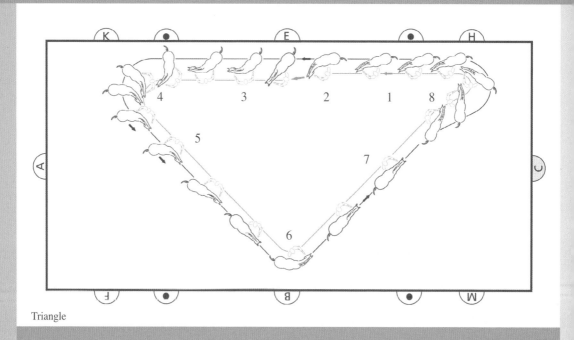

Triangle

imaginery triangle. When you are on the out-side, the following combination is possible: on the long side, move the horse from counter-shoulder-in to travers, pirouette at the end of the first side then allow the horse to walk straight across the next side, followed by a quarter-circle to the third diagonal which is completed as a half-pass. A tight travers turn completes the triangle.

It is important that the horse is straightened on one of the diagonals, so no impulsion is lost between the lateral movements and the turns.

Square figures of eight

The square figure of eight is a continuation of the work done on the square circle. It is very useful to connect lateral movements and pirouettes.

Begin in counter-shoulder-in (1), but not with too great an angle – it should be on three tracks so that the turn on the quarters in the counter-bend (2) can be carried out correctly.

It is important to ensure the horse is moving well forwards, otherwise the inside foreleg will not be able to cross over in front of the other one and the horse may stumble or step behind the outside fore instead. After this the horse's shoulders return to the line of the square to straighten (3). Before the corner, bend the horse away from you so that the quarter-circle in the corner (4) prepares for the half-pass down the third side (5).

At the end of this side lift the forehand and prepare him for the quarter pirouette around the inside hindleg that follows (6). Half-pass follows on the fourth side (7). At the end

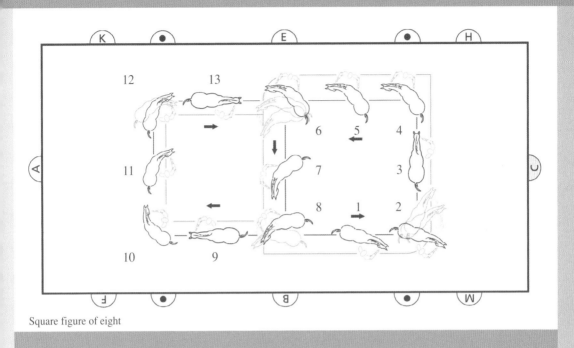

Square figure of eight

of this side keep control of the shoulders whilst at the same time encouraging the quarters to engage, so that the change of direction into renvers can be completed (8). This change should only be done for two to three steps so the horse can immediately then be straightened (9).

Now the handler is positioned on the inside of the square and to the inside of the horse. A quarter-circle follows (10), which prepares for the following movement. As you come out of the quarter-circle, allow the horse's shoulders go come in slightly (11) so that the shoulder-in is created down this side. A turn on the forehand in the shoulder-in position completes the next corner (12). A straight line completes the final side of the eight to be continued as wished.

Combining lateral exercises using the entire manege

All of the lateral movements learnt to date can be combined to use the entire manege. Parts of this can be taken out and incorporated in everyday work.

In order to avoid the so-called 'lateral syndrome' in which the horse doesn't have the ability to go in a straight line, great value must be place from the start on straightness. This is why all combinations of movements will include phases where the horse must go straight.

From the short side go deep into the corner (1). The horse should be clearly flexed and bent and move smoothly into the shoulder-in (2).

So that you can always guarantee to be able to bring the horse away from the outside track,

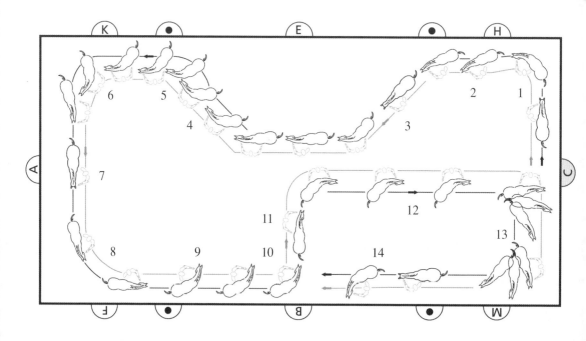

Combining lateral exercises using the entire manege

after the shoulder-in go onto a short diagonal (3) where the horse is straightened and then flexed away from the handler to prepare perfectly for the half-pass (4) which follows.

From the half-pass, move into the renvers (5). The horse's forehand shouldn't meet the outside track but instead is kept off the track to the inside. In the following quarter-circle in renvers (6) the horse is still bent away from the handler. The quarters are describing a larger circle than the forehand. The second short side is used to straighten the horse again (7). In the next corner the horse

should be flexed and bent to the inside (8), to then move into shoulder-in on the long side (9).

At B (10) turn in towards the centre using the straight line and following quarter circle (11) to prepare for the travers to follow (12). Continue this until just before the outside track on the short side following this with two quarter pirouettes (13) to finish on the long side.

On the long side, straighten the horse on the inside track and finish the exercise with a counter-shoulder-in (14).

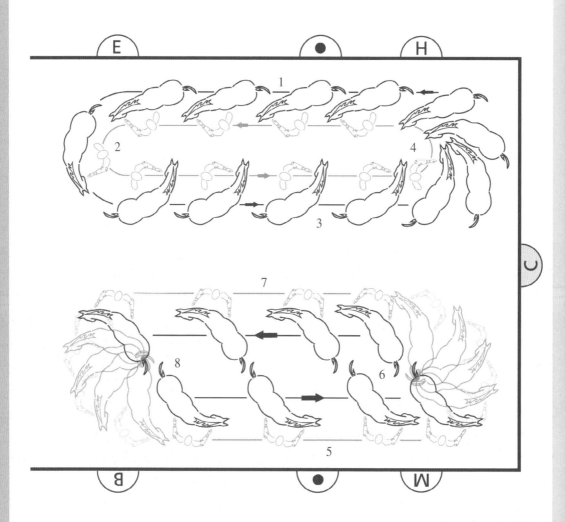

Combined work

Combined work

Further combinations using lateral movements are shown here. It is important not to forget to allow the horse to take a break between exercises to go forwards in an active walk.

1. Shoulder-in on three tracks
2. Half ten-metre circle
3. Counter-shoulder-in on four tracks
4. Turn on the half-circle
5. Travers
6. Pirouette
7. Renvers
8. Pirouette

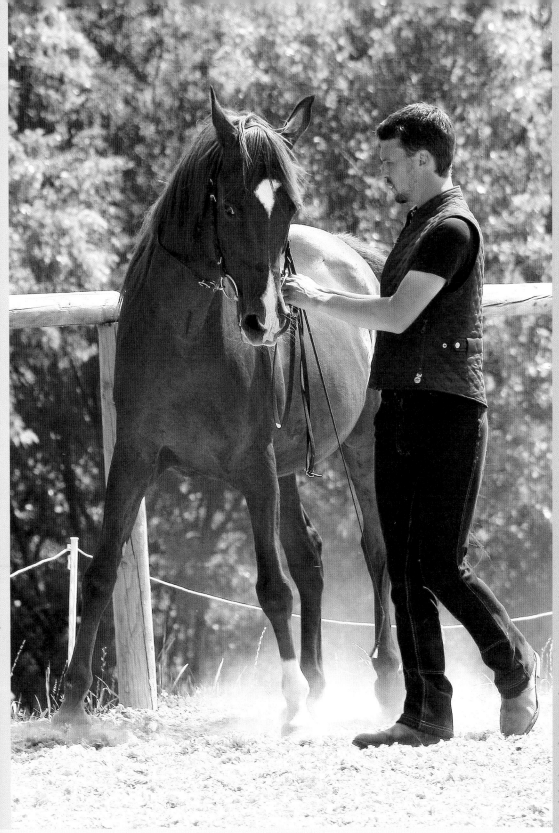

Thanks to careful preparation the supple horse can complete all lateral movements.

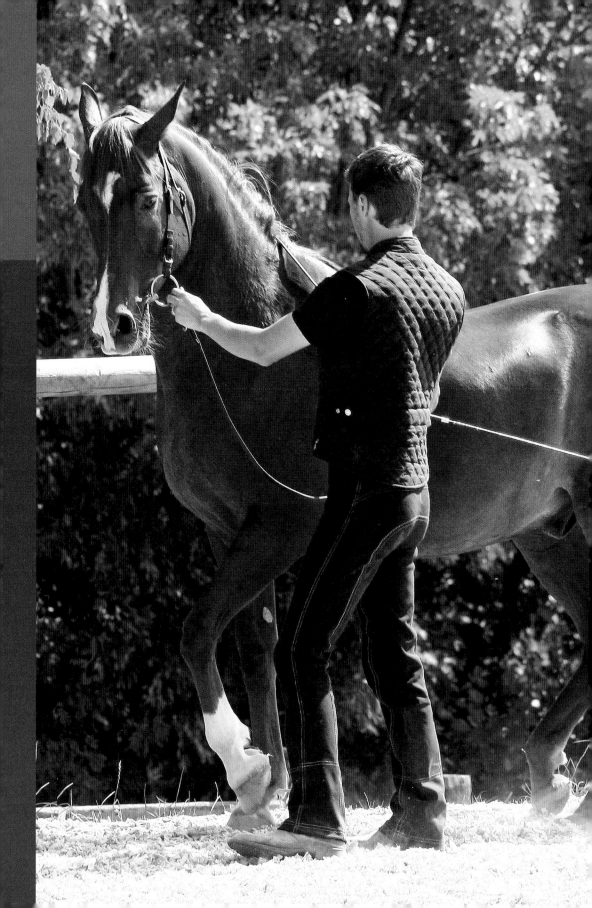

Advanced work

Expression and enjoyment

As the advanced work continues, the comm-unication with your horse will become increas-ingly finer and subtler, with the aids through the reins becoming no more than a vibration. The horse will go forwards in self-carriage. The outline will become rounder and he will sit back on his haunches.

Horse and trainer will have gained experi-ence and a certain routine through the training process, with mistakes being minimised and the difficult work towards collection can be started. There are a large number of exercises by which the horse is taught to work through his quarters more and raise his forehand. Again, it should not be forgotten that the advanced exercises are not done for their own sake, but rather are a means to an end. Improved balance enables the horse to sit on his haunches and become lighter in the forehand. In the exercis-es working towards collection, the handler's ambition is usually to the cost of the horse. A perfect piaffe doesn't necessarily have to be the end result. Not every horse is physically suited to do this. At the end of the day you should always work towards the horse enjoy-ing himself and showing expression in his work, whether in lateral movements or high collection.

GROUNDWORK FOR BAROQUE HORSES

Baroque horses are not born sitting on their quarters – baroque breeds also have to build-up and develop the muscles needed for collection.

In-hand work is ideally suited to straight-ening the horse and encouraging him to follow the rein down, before working towards more collected work. Eventually, thanks to the physical advantages of the baroque horse, this leads to perfection in the advanced movements of the High School work.

Transition from walk to trot in shoulder-in
The right moment to trot is just as the horse's outside hind leg is suspended above the ground. The inside hind is the weight-bearing leg and will next be stepping forward under his body. Flexion and bend in the shoulder-in are correct, the inside hip will lower at the next step and gives the hind leg its direction.

The handler himself needs to walk confidently forward, giving the voice command and using the whip in order to encourage the inside leg to step through. At the same time the whip creates the tension needed to move into trot.

Transitions

In order to multiply the advantages of the effects of the lateral movements, transitions from walk to trot can be introduced to the work.

Lateral movements in trot
When trot is brought into lateral movements, the angle must not be changed. In trot the horse should maintain the same quality in the movement as in the walk. It is important to watch which hind leg the horse uses first in the new pace. In shoulder-in and counter-shoulder-in, the inside hind should be activated first; in travers, renvers and half-pass, it should be the outside hind.

By this stage the voice should be the only aid needed to be used to ask the horse to trot. The whip can be used on the appropriate hind leg to support the voice. The timing of the commands is very important, so the horse starts to trot as the hind leg is about to swing forwards.

At this point a diagonal pair of legs steps forwards and the horse, maintaining his bend and flexion, moves into shoulder-in in trot.

This means that the hips are positioned correctly to ensure that the sideways movement is maintained.

Downwards transitions

The transition from trot to walk while in shoulder-in must also be carefully watched. The trot is a two-beat pace, which means that diagonal pairs of legs must move regularly and in sequence.

The correct moment for the transition is when the inside hind leg leaves the ground. At exactly this moment the flow of the movement is unchanged and the shoulder-in can be continued at the walk. The half-halt consists of a number of stages combined. The outside rein prepares the horse for the walk – small, gentle half-halts get the horse's attention, the inside rein can also be gently taken up, ensuring that the bend isn't altered. Next a voice command

1

Transition from trot to walk in shoulder-in

The preparation for the transition is complete – the horse is swinging in a regular trot with the inside hind leg moving forward, but ready to change to the walk. The final half-halt keeps the horse on his inside hind leg somewhat longer so that he moves into walk.

Here the walk is clearly recognisable. The handler's hand follows the horse's head in a slightly lower position as the frame in walk must be a bit longer than in the trot. The hand should allow the neck room to stretch at the point of transition. The flexion and bend of the shoulder-in needs to be maintained, and allows the inside hind leg to step under the body in the transition.

2

The rhythm of the walk is established and the horse maintains the shoulder-in position and continues with it in walk. It is very important that during the transition the inside rein is not pulled back, as this might cause the horse to tilt his head. The picture shows that the inside rein is never pulled back, but instead supports the outside.

is given and the handler's upper body is drawn up and back. The voice can also be used to re-inforce the outside rein's call to attention.

Swing

Another exercise that works towards collection is the swing (also called rocker or see-saw). In order to get the most out of this exercise the horse needs to be able to fulfill the follow prerequisites which make up the exercise:

1. Measured walk
2. Collected halt
3. Rein-back.

The swing is an alternating forwards and back-wards movement which in due course can be developed so that in the rein-back the horse's centre of gravity is moved back towards the haunches in order then to use them to move forwards.

The handler needs to constantly refine his own body language so that eventually a slight pulling back of the upper body will suffice to ask for the rein-back. The upper body moving forwards should then cause the horse to move forwards. If you shorten the time between the forwards and backwards movements, then out of this you get the beginnings of movement on the spot – the piaffe.

1. Measured walk

A milestone of the gymnastic in-hand work is the very slow, measured walk. Each individual step must be controlled and determined by the handler, with the horse trading a path between slowness and purposeful.

The horse must next learn to slow his tempo down following the least amount of pressure on the rein. The handler's hand should barely vibrate the rein – no more, no less. These small signals get the horse's attention; at first he may think that he is being asked to halt and react accordingly. The whip should be used to continue the forwards movement and make it clear that he should slow his tempo and not change pace – there is a fine distinction between the two, and the degree will vary from horse to horse.

This vibration must be minimal, the handler almost 'shivering' with his lower arm to give fine signals up to the bit, working from bottom to top so that the horse's frame also lifts, while the walk slows.

In this way the horse learns to recognise very subtle aids, which lift and hold the forehand.

The second component of the walk is the purpose of the walk through the quarters. At the start it is enough to send the horse on if he tries to halt so that he slows his walk but doesn't stand. This is the job of the whip initially.

Once the horse understands the aids through the reins and responds promptly and lightly, the driving whip aid takes on a greater importance. Now it is time to create more energy from behind. The whip needs to be used in the same way as the aforementioned rein aids, vibrating to energise his quarters – it is not a matter of touching individual legs but rather of activating the entire hindquarters. As soon as the horse responds and the tempo through the quarters is increased, the use of the whip should cease and the horse should be praised.

One to three active steps are enough at first. If the horse reacts too much forwards, it will be felt through the reins. The voice should be used to calm whilst at the same time increasing the intensity of the vibrating aids through the reins until the horse comes back to a slower walk.

Initially a lot of patience is needed until the horse understands what is being asked of him, but soon you will be able to count the measured walk amongst his repertoire of exercises.

2. Collected walk

Once the measured walk has been learnt, a halt out of this will create a collected halt. If this doesn't happen, it is possible to lift the outline in halt as he will understand the aid through the rein moving up towards the corner of his mouth. Ideally the collected halt should come out of the collected walk.

3. Rein-back

From the collected halt the handler has to simply turn his upper body in slightly towards the horse using the same small half-halts as in the walk, and indicate the new direction of the movement.

Your legs should be placed slightly wider apart so that you can transfer your own weight correctly. From this position ask for one or two

From the measured walk ...

... comes the halt: one leads to the other.

The handler's body language is the most important aid for the swing exercise. At collected walk you can recognise the basic position, although the whip is held horizontally at this stage of training so that the right degree of tension is created. The handler's body is facing the horse.

steps back. The voice should support this with a command that will have already been learnt. The horse's head must not tip behind the vertical when in the rein-back. He should transfer his weight back and not just rush backwards.

The goals

Once the horse has learnt these three steps, then he is ready to carry out the swing exercise. He should be light in the forehand and be collected without being compressed. The preparatory exercises are ideally suited to

sit the horse on his haunches whilst staying in self-carriage. Thanks to the collected rein-back the horse's balance is transferred more to the hindquarters and the much sought after lightening and lifting of the forehand will quickly become a reality, supporting the muscular development of the entire body.

A further goal arises out of the increasingly subtle communication between horse and handler. The aids are reduced to a minimum.

As well as learning balance, the swing trains his ability to pay attention. The smallest com-

For the rein-back, it should now suffice for the handler's upper body to be moved in the direction of the required movement. The aids through the bit must be precise, but light and subtle. Thanks to his widened stance, the handler can transfer his own weight either forwards or backwards. The horse must also be able to transfer his weight. Only a few steps are needed before the whip should be ready to send the horse on again forwards.

mand from the handler must be recognised by the horse and responded to. On the other hand, the handler needs to learn to control his own body and ensure that he doesn't give any un-intentional signals.

The handler's upper body send the signals to start forwards, the whip enlivens the hindquarters, with the bit filtering out any excess forwards thrust from the horse. The hindquarters step forward with shortened strides. Following this comes halt, rein-back and forwards. Over time the interval between transitions can become shorter and shorter, so that move-ment almost on the spot is developed – from here, the piaffe is not far off.

Outlook

Where to next?

Once you have read this book you will have the basic knowledge to enrich and improve your horse's life. Health is one of life's most valuable commodities – not only for us, but for the horse as well – and often it takes very little to make a big difference.

As far back as the Romans, it was acknowledged that a healthy mind can only live in a healthy body. And this is exactly what can be achieved with the help of in-hand work. Freed from a rider's weight, the horse can be trained precisely as wished, needing no particular talent to learn this type of work and yet potentially leading to astonishing results.

Once the basic lessons have been learnt and can be carried out, it is no great distance to doing these under saddle. The horse's expression, pride and dignity cannot be touched – the harmony that has been reached will continue into the ridden work.

If you concentrate on preserving the understanding already attained, then the manege becomes a playground, a place where horse and rider feel at home, a fitness centre for the horse where the less competitive rider can

The half-pass learnt in-hand can also be ridden with real expression.

A gymnastically trained horse often finds his strengths in forwards movements …

also enjoy the thrill of riding a half-pass.

Usually a horse's training will come to a halt at a certain level. Only exceptional horses are seen as having the potential for High School work and lateral movements. Leisure riders who can't afford horses with such potential often just give up, along the lines of 'Stick to what you are comfortable with'. Despite this, there is a demand for a training method that can be easily followed, and can help support and improve your horse without exceeding your own or your horse's ability.

With passion to unknown heights

The in-hand training described here is done without training aids or gadgets. Nothing is

…and in collected movements. Perfection isn't everything, but expression is.

used to hide faults or create a false impression. The path is a long one, but as a trainer you have the chance to recognise the exact strengths and weaknesses of your horse and to respond to them accordingly.

The horse's conformation and his mind determine both the path and direction taken with his training. The lateral work can be learnt by, and benefit, any horse, but the collected movements may be out of the reach of some.

During the horse's education it will be clear which exercises suit him and where there are difficulties. In any case, thanks to the unforced work based on understanding, any horse will be allowed to show his latent talent.

The greatest challenge is the start. The basic work will decide whether it will be a success or a failure. The better and more thorough the horse is schooled in-hand, the easier all the following exercises will be. No hour invested in the basics is a wasted one, but rather creates the physical and mental pre-conditions for improvement.

Your own horse may not be a wonder of extravagant movement. He doesn't need to be, as in truth it is not a matter of spectacular talent that nature – or rather breeding – has bestowed, but rather of what is inside every horse: expression, enthusiasm and joy in his own movement.

Every horse learns within his own limitations to achieve a degree of mobility and suppleness that may lead him to unsuspected heights. The enthusiasm and passion that can be developed with in-hand work can sooner or later be found in a horse's face.

Everyone makes mistakes, and there is no shame in this. The greatest advantage of in-hand work is that you are quicker to recognise these mistakes. You have the whole horse in your field of vision and you are not reliant only on feel. When you sit in the saddle but have never ridden a correct shoulder-in, it is very hard to know when it is right. Even with the support of an experienced instructor, the lateral movements often pose a big question for horse and rider. In addition, most of the time you are schooling alone and the knowledge of what is correct is replaced by guess work.

In-hand work is quite different. You can see the horse's shoulders, the angles, the bend, the energy through the quarters, and correct the mistakes of both horse and handler immediately.

Through constantly striving for improved balance, progress is made much faster, albeit differently for every horse. In some it will be a wonderful half-pass, in others an expressive piaffe or collected canter. But even the simplest of turns will make a horse more supple and flexible.

Extended trot, for obvious reasons, doesn't belong to in-hand work, as the handler just couldn't keep up. Despite this, thanks to the improved balance created by the work described here, the ability to extend is improved. The thrust from the hindquarters is naturally part of every horse as a flight animal, and the ability to set his weight more through his quarters built-up by gymnastic exercises enhances this ability, and can hugely improve the paces.

Badly ridden or spoilt horses, thanks to the retraining of the muscles, can achieve a sense of balance that allows them to carry a rider's weight again confidently. Resistance that often arises from pain caused from blockages in muscles disappears. In-hand work is no guarantee for a healthy horse, but is a valuable aid to keeping your four-legged friend healthy.

FURTHER EXERCISES FOR THE ADVANCED HORSE

Collected lateral movements

What starts with measured walk ends with consistent training towards collection without the need for strong hands. Lateral work in collected walk or trot have an effect on the entire musculature of the horse.

The top line will build up, over time creating a superbly rounded outline from withers to poll, and with an ability to really sit on his haunches.

Further transitions

Transitions between halt and trot, or from rein-back to trot and halt, strengthen the quarters and turn the forwards thrust into an ability to bear more weight behind.

The positive tension and the muscle tone of the horse will be increased and he will gain energy.

Piaffe

From the swing exercise can be developed a collected trot, which can turn into piaffe. The transition between halt and trot can also lead in this direction.

Collected canter

If the horse canters on a volte and then goes straight, a supple horse may also be schooled in-hand in canter. In canter, the horse must put his weight back through his quarters, in order not to create too many difficulties for his handler.

Levade

The ultimate outcome of the ability to transfer his weight through his hindquarters for any horse is in the levade. In this lesson the horse must be able to bear his entire weight on his hind legs.

The leading man

Malcolm's story

The last part of this book is dedicated to a horse that is proof of the usefulness of in-hand work.

A pure-bred Arab, Malcolm had many problems in his youth. As a three-year-old he started to develop a sway back without ever having been ridden.

Despite exhaustive examinations, the cause for this could never be determined. The opinion of various vets was clear: Malcolm could never be ridden, as his back would not bear the strain.

In order to enable him to live a comfortable life and possibly one day be ridden, a therapy of steroids and training on the lunge with side reins was prescribed.

Neither had the desired results, in fact quite the opposite. By the time he was four, Malcolm was experiencing significant pain in his lumbar vertebrae and his hips that, due to his sway back and the absence of any supporting musculature, were severely strained.

Rescue and transformation

Thanks to treatment by an outstanding vet using chiropractic treatment and acupuncture, the most serious causes of pain were treated, and Malcolm could lead a life free from pain. At the same time work was begun with gymnastic exercises in-hand which were essential for his full recovery. Circus lessons completed the work.

This gradual training was an astounding success. Not only was Malcolm without pain,

Malcolm at the age of four years.

Whether on the lunge …

he was also strong enough to be ridden gently in walk some months later. His musculature built up, and his movement became surer. The sway back stayed, but it was supported by a strengthened body underneath it.

Until this point Malcolm had been an introvert and physically not at all equipped to cope with collected work. Malcolm's low self-esteem and his low rank in the herd didn't make him an obvious candidate for High School work.

Despite this, lateral work led him into a world where he felt increasingly comfortable. Patience and time – two elements which were imperative for his training – allowed his muscles to gradually build up, enabling him to start towards collection.

From here things moved quickly. With every month, Malcolm became more sure of himself and more expressive in his work. Thanks to the collected exercises, his top line developed, he became stronger and stronger, enjoying his life as a self-confident horse both in-hand and under saddle. From the introverted little Arab grew a wonderful, safe horse, sure of himself, and despite his sway back, able to find his place in High School work.

During his career Malcolm has learnt to bow, curtsey, sit and lie down. The Spanish walk has become his favourite and makes him very light in the forehand.

Here I would like to give my thanks to this very special horse. It was his exceptional transformation that was the inspiration for this book and made me hope that many other horses would follow in his path to health and self-confidence.

… or working free …

… in hand …

… or when ridden: Malcolm has become a healthy and proud horse.

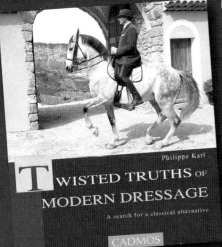